Delight in the Day

Delight
IN THE
Day

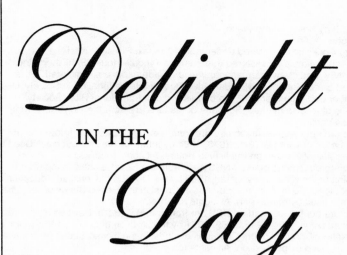

"THIS IS THE DAY
WHICH THE LORD HATH MADE;
WE WILL REJOICE AND BE GLAD IN IT."
Psalm 118:24

Shirley Pope Waite

Tyndale House Publishers, Inc.
Wheaton, Illinois

Library of Congress Cataloging-in-Publication Data
Waite, Shirley Pope, date
Delight in the day / Shirley Pope Waite.
p.cm.
ISBN 0-8423-1216-1. — ISBN 0-8423-1217-X (pbk.)
1. Family—Prayer-books and devotions—English. I. Title.
BV255.W34 1993
242—dc2093-12912

Printed in the United States of America
99 98 97 96 95 94 93
8   7   6   5   4   3   2   1

To my husband, Kyle, without whose love, patience, and encouragement this book would not have become a reality

Contents

CHAPTER ONE
Delight in Family *1*

CHAPTER TWO
Delight in Travel *35*

CHAPTER THREE
Delight in Everyday Saints *69*

CHAPTER FOUR
Delight in Values *97*

CHAPTER FIVE
Delight in Holidays *131*

CHAPTER SIX
Delight in Friendship *159*

CHAPTER SEVEN
Delight in God's Word *187*

CHAPTER EIGHT
Delight in Oneself *217*

CHAPTER NINE
Delight in Nature *247*

CHAPTER TEN
Delight in Prayer *281*

CHAPTER ELEVEN
Delight in Worship and Praise *311*

CHAPTER TWELVE
Delight in Sharing with Youngsters *341*

CHAPTER THIRTEEN
Delight in the ABCs *377*

Delight in Family

If there is righteousness in the heart,
there will be beauty in the character.
If there be beauty in the character,
there will be harmony in the home.
If there is harmony in the home,
there will be order in the nation.
When there is order in the nation,
there will be peace in the world.

—Author Unknown

Making Ripples

Take heed therefore, that the light which is in thee be not darkness.   (Luke 11:35)

"I'll find a better skipper than you do!"

I can still hear my sons trying to outdo each other on the shores of Flathead Lake. The stones on that Montana beach come in all shapes and sizes. When wet, they are among the most beautiful I've ever seen.

But the boys were mainly interested in flat saucer-like stones that skip along the surface of the water when thrown with a sidearm movement. Each wanted to outdo the other, but their mutual goal was to best Dad's record.

The children also enjoyed watching the ripples, to see if any traveled all the way to shore.

We are like skipping stones touching the water's surface. As we touch another life, we make ripples. It may be a light ripple that stays with the person all day. A deeper "touch down" might result in ripples that travel with another for years!

What an awesome responsibility—making ripples! Right now, I'm trying to send ripples of love to a newly divorced woman in my church, ripples of justice to a son who has been mistreated on a job, ripples of joy to a neighbor who has become reconciled to a wayward daughter. Do you need to send out ripples of God's light to someone?

PRAYER:
Lord, I want to share your light and send out ripples of your love. Help me, please. Amen.

🙐 *TODAY'S DELIGHT:*
Find a way to affirm <u>uncle Harrell</u>
(name of a person) today by a ripple of
<u>comfort + love</u> *(what the person needs most).*

An Unbirthday Cake

Serve one another in love.   (Galatians 5:13 NIV)

A white cake with lemon filling and fudge frosting. That's my husband's favorite kind, so I usually bake one for his birthday.

A few years ago, after a bitter disagreement, I wanted to apologize to my husband but couldn't voice it. That's when I decided to make him an "unbirthday" cake. It was, of course, white with lemon filling and fudge frosting. Other occasions of a happier nature arose—a promotion, an almost-perfect bowling score, and recently, his return from a special men's retreat. The "unbirthday" cake helped me to say, "I love and missed you" with tangible (and yummy) evidence.

Do you sometimes have trouble communicating your feelings? You might want to bake an "unbirthday" cake. Or you could prepare your loved one's favorite breakfast or dinner. On the other hand, your "unbirthday" gift need not cost a thing. You might polish your husband's shoes, type your teenager's overdue term paper, or simply dry the dishes for your wife.

A nice thing about "unbirthday" gifts—they're appropriate 364 days of the year!

An Unbirthday Cake

PRAYER:
Father, I want to give an "unbirthday" gift to
_____. I'm open to your suggestions right
now.

• *TODAY'S DELIGHT:*
Follow through with an "unbirthday" cake or gift for
someone you love. (See my recipe on the next page.)

My Unbirthday Cake Recipe

First prepare and bake your favorite white cake mix (one with pudding in the mix is best) in two greased round layer cake pans. Spread lemon filling between cooled layers (recipe below). Then frost with fudge frosting (recipe also below).

Lemon Filling
    3/4 cup sugar
    2 tablespoons cornstarch
    dash of salt
    1 slightly beaten egg yolk
    3/4 cup water
    3 tablespoons lemon juice (bottled lemon juice
        works fine)
    1 tablespoon butter
    1 teaspoon grated lemon peel (optional)

Mix sugar, cornstarch, and salt. Add egg yolk, water, and lemon juice. Cook until thick, stirring constantly. Remove from heat. Add peel and butter. Cool before spreading between layers. (Or cook in microwave three minutes, stirring after each minute.)

Fudge Frosting
    2 cups sugar
    1 cup water
    1/4 teaspoon salt
    2 one-ounce squares
        (or packets)
    unsweetened chocolate
    2 tablespoons corn syrup
    2 tablespoons butter
    1 teaspoon vanilla

My Unbirthday Cake Recipe

Cook sugar, water, salt, chocolate, and corn syrup over low heat, stirring constantly until sugar dissolves. Continue cooking to soft-ball stage (236 degrees F). Remove from heat. Add butter and cool to lukewarm. Add vanilla and beat until mixture is of spreading consistency. Spread quickly on cake. If frosting becomes too stiff, add a few drops of hot water or place pan on low heat for a few seconds. (This recipe can be adapted for a microwave. Check any microwave recipe for fudge.)

≥● *TODAY'S DELIGHT:*
A piece of "unbirthday" cake!

Skibicki

Maybe you've noticed the invisible presence of a gremlin named "Not Me" in the delightful comic strip *Family Circus.* "Not Me" is the one who doesn't put toys away and scribbles on Daddy's papers. My mother used to call these annoyances "come done" happenings.

Not long after we were married, I discovered we had an invisible "fall guy" residing in our apartment. His name was "Skibicki."

I'd find cracker crumbs on the coffee table. "Skibicki did it," my husband would calmly explain. My complaints of dirty socks on the bathroom floor elicited the comment, "Skibicki must have left them there."

When our children came along, Skibicki was a firmly established member of the Waite household. The kids were quick to get acquainted with him.

I remember a three year old surveying a puddle of spilled milk on the floor. He solemnly looked me in the eye and said, "Bicki did it!"

Skibicki tracked in mud, got fingerprints on clean guest towels, and ate the last of the strawberries I'd planned for dessert.

Sometimes Skibicki took a vacation. If teenagers used too much gas in the family car, tools were missing, or a window was broken, things got tense.

But if our beloved "fall guy" rejoined the family circle, the dastardly deed did not seem so awful.

The kids are gone now, but I'm really glad Skibicki hasn't left. Just the other day my husband decided to try the timer on our new coffeemaker prior to our running an errand. When we returned, freshly brewed coffee was dripping off the counter and running down the side of the stove onto the floor. He'd forgotten to put the carafe under the filter basket. Before I had a chance to rant and rave, Kyle piped up, "I'll bet Skibicki's been here!" We were soon grabbing paper towels together, laughing uproariously.

Imperfect wives live with imperfect husbands. Imperfect parents raise imperfect children. It's easy to blame somebody else when things go wrong. Our pride keeps us from admitting failure, so we turn into harping, complaining individuals.

Of course, we must face up to our mistakes, but a God-given sense of humor often defuses an otherwise explosive situation. Fortunate are the families who have a "Skibicki" hiding around the corner, taking the brunt of those "come done" incidents that are part of family living.

(Apologies to any reader whose last name happens to be Skibicki. We love you!)

&❧ *TODAY'S DELIGHT:*
Whatever goes wrong today, try to see the humor in it, and if possible, laugh it off. You may even want to invite

*a "Skibicki" into your home for a visit. Don't be
surprised if he or she becomes a permanent resident.*

Weirdo, DingFratas, and Snickle-fritz

What's in a name?
That which we call a rose
By any other name would smell as sweet.
                    —William Shakespeare (1564–1616)

Since the kids have left home, I miss the sounds of some of the family nicknames that used to pepper the air.

I remember when our daughter invited a college friend home for the weekend. As she bounced into the house, she greeted her father, "Hi, Weirdo!"

When she saw the shocked expression on her friend's face, she hastily added, "Oh, it's not how it sounds!"

I don't know where the term came from or how it got started, but *Weirdo* became a word of endearment at our house.

My husband used to have a difficult time expressing audible affection to the children, and was never much of a "kid cuddler." But they knew their dad loved them by the good-natured nicknames he gave them—when he'd throw a stick of gum across the room to the youngest and call out, "Catch, DingFratas!"—when he'd surprise the oldest with a case of oil for his car and say, "I've got something out on the patio for you, Snickle-fritz!"—when he called

Laurie at college and opened the conversation with "Hi, Weirdo. How's everything going?"

Strange as it may seem, when that term was missing, I'd become aware of tension in our home. But when the "Weirdo"s filled the air, I knew all was well.

Laurie is now a married woman and lives in Ohio, but occasionally, via long-distance, she or her dad will address the other affectionately, "Hi Weirdo."

❧ *TODAY'S DELIGHT:*
Enjoy the pet names in your family. They are translated, "I care about you."

Keep On Loving

But God proves his love for us in that while we still were sinners Christ died for us.   (Romans 5:8 NRSV)

"Why do we still bother?" my husband asked glumly.

Why bother, indeed? We'd been giving and giving to our younger son, and as far as we could tell, he didn't appreciate it. He never wrote and only called when a problem arose or he needed financial assistance. I'd lost track of how many CARE packages we mailed or sent with friends who visited his city. How many checks went unacknowledged, yet showed up in our bank statements? How many self-addressed stamped envelopes were never used? Yes, I thought dejectedly, why did we still bother?

Could God say the same thing about me? Do I fail to show appreciation, carelessly taking his provisions for granted? How often do I turn to him only when I'm facing a problem? Could his heart be saddened, just as my heart breaks when I don't hear from my son?

I have loved this child since I first became aware of his presence within my body. God loved me while I was yet a sinner, and chose me before the foundation of the world (Ephesians 1:4).

I paused and then answered meekly, "I guess because he's our child and we love him."

14

PRAYER:
Thank you, Lord, for proving your love
unconditionally, and for dying for me.

🍂 *TODAY'S DELIGHT:*
Drop a card to a loved one. Simply say, "I'm thinking of
you and want you to know I love you."

Standing in the Gap

*I looked in vain for anyone who . . . could stand in
the gap . . . but I found not one.* (Ezekiel 22:30 TLB)

My memory is short. For weeks after I'd written the
previous devotion, I continued to "bloody my
knuckles on the door of heaven." That's when the
Lord gave me the following words. I share them,
hoping they will challenge you as they have me.

> *I'll stand in the gap for my son.*
> *I'll stand 'til the victory's won.*
> > *This one thing I know*
> > *That You love him so,*
> *And Your work with my child is not done.*

> *I'll stand in the gap every day,*
> *And there I will fervently pray;*
> > *And, Lord, just one favor,*
> > *Don't let me waver*
> *If things get quite rough, which they may.*

> *I'll never give up on that boy.*
> *Nor will You, for You promised him joy.*
> > *For I know it was true*
> > *When he said "Yes" to You,*
> *Though the enemy seeks to destroy.*

> *I'll not quit as I intercede,*
> *For You are his Savior, indeed!*

Though it may take years,
I give You my fears,
As I trust every moment I plead.

And so in the gap I will stand,
Heeding Your every command,
With help from above,
I unconditionally love,
And soon he will reach for Your hand.

PRAYER:
Lord, keep reminding me—over and over—to stand in the gap.

❧ *TODAY'S DELIGHT:*
Post a snapshot of your child, spouse, parent, or friend on your bathroom mirror, above the kitchen sink, or on your desk. Whenever you look at it, say to yourself, "I'm standing in the gap for you."

Table Grace and Tears

*He [Paul] took some bread and gave thanks to
God in front of them all.* (Acts 27:35 NIV)

I always felt awkward eating at my children's homes.
None of them continued the family tradition of saying
grace before meals. However, they invariably asked
my husband or me to give thanks. We usually recited
words handed down from my English grandparents:

> For what we are about to receive,
> May the Lord make us truly thankful. Amen.

A sweet granddaughter became part of our family
circle and was soon old enough to join her parents at
mealtime. On a recent visit, we gathered around the
oak table for supper. Mark first glanced at his wife,
then at his dad and me. Obviously embarrassed, he
explained, "I hope you folks won't be offended, but
we've decided to use Anne's family blessing. First, we
hold hands."

We reached out to each other, and Jessica repeated
with her parents:

> Come, Lord Jesus, be our Guest,
> And let Thy gifts to us be blest. Amen.

I didn't join the others audibly in asking God's
blessing that day. Tears were too close to the surface,

and the lump in my throat was too large. But I ate joyfully!

PRAYER:

> God is great, God is good,
> Let us thank Him for our food. Amen.

    ❧ *TODAY'S DELIGHT:*
Look up and introduce a new grace to say at mealtime.

Waves and Smiles

At all times make it your aim to do good to one another and to all people. (1 Thessalonians 5:15 TEV)

We'd never been alone with our two-year-old granddaughter. Would she fuss about an hour's drive without her parents? We securely strapped Jessica into her car seat at the back of our motor home. I immediately drew her attention to the books her daddy handed me before we pulled out of the driveway.

I'd forgotten the short attention span of a two year old. Jessica brushed aside *Go, Dog, Go!* and the other books, asking for Mommy. I pointed to trees, mountains, and moving traffic through the back window, trying to divert her attention. Just about the time her face began to cloud over, a man in the car directly behind us waved. Jessica was fascinated and waved back. He passed us and when the next car approached, Jessica initiated the waving. The rest of the trip went smoothly with her newfound game.

When my children were growing up, we waved to train engineers, bus drivers, the checkout clerk, and people crossing the street as we waited for a light.[1]

As I've grown older, I sometimes neglect the simple

[1] A sad commentary on our society: We must be cautious and pray for discernment regarding friendly gestures to strangers, especially where children are concerned.

courtesy of a smile or a wave. I must correct that today! I'll start by waving to the trash collector I see outside my window.

PRAYER:
Lord, loosen up my arm and my smile muscles so that my warmth may make a difference in someone's life today.

🙢 *TODAY DELIGHT:*
Be generous with your smiles and waves today.

High School Reunion

My husband was apprehensive.
It was his first high school reunion—the fortieth.
"Nobody will recognize me!"
From across the room, a voice boomed, "If it isn't
Kyle Waite! He walks just like his dad!"
A deeper voice jokingly echoed, "I thought it was his
ugly brother!"
A strong family resemblance saved Kyle from
embarrassment.
What an eye-opener—that reunion!
Classmates sought out a familiar wide grin . . .
A long-remembered whimsical sense of humor . . .
A fellow band member—or football player.
They chose to ignore the physical changes (and there
were many!).

I think of the characteristics by which old friends
knew my husband.
He walked like his dad.
Do I walk in God's pathways?
He resembled his brother.
Do I resemble my brother, Jesus? I have little choice
about the aging process in my body.
But with the Lord's help, I can guard my spirit from
atrophy.

🐦 *TODAY'S DELIGHT:*
Contact by phone or letter a high school friend, college classmate, or other friend from the past.

A Brother Remembers

My only brother and I were reminiscing over the phone one day. Among his vivid memories was a time when he was hospitalized and I'd come home from the West to visit.

"I remember hugging you and how you stiffened up," he said.

I hadn't recalled the episode; nevertheless, I felt guilty and later wrote a letter of apology. His answer came promptly.

"Do you remember being my 'surrogate' mother in my preschool days? You taught me how to tell time, how to button my coat, how to tie my shoes. You taught me the words to 'Silent Night,' and how to recite 'ladybug, ladybug, fly away home.' You pushed me on an old, large tricycle because I couldn't reach the pedals and played 'Store' with me, using old bottles and tin cans.

"You took me to school my first year and watched out for me. Later, you helped me with my homework and were instrumental in my winning my first spelling bee. I remember how you drilled me in the multiplication tables one summer by using flash cards. Remember? I passed math on the condition I would learn multiplication over the summer.

"And what about the times you took me to the Saturday matinees and let me ride your girl's bike because the folks couldn't afford another bike?

"If these things don't demonstrate love, what does, my dear big sister?"

As I read the words, tears welled up in my eyes, and healing began in my heart.

Thank you, dear brother, for helping me to see that love is expressed in many different ways.

  TODAY'S DELIGHT:
Contact a sibling or other relative (or even a friend) and talk about the times when he or she showed you special love in the past.

Red (and Pink) Roses
for a Blue Lady

The highest reaches of the hilltop to the depths of the valley!

We'd driven across the state to attend the baptism of a precious four-month-old grandson and were delighted that our son and family had become actively involved in their church.

We returned home to find a devastating message on the answering machine. My thirty-one-year-old nephew had taken his own life! I was too far away to offer comfort to my brother except by phone.

Then during the week, my local church refused to take a stand on a controversial issue. I began to feel like Elijah, "I am the only one left!" (1 Kings 19:10 NIV).

The inevitable happened. I became increasingly difficult to live with. Thursday, my husband asked, "What *is* the matter with you?"

"I'm in grief! For my brother and for our church! Leave me alone!" Friday, he handed me a dozen red and pink roses. The card read, "Because you've had such a rough week, and just because you're you! I love you!"

Did I immediately snap out of it? Sad to say, that Saturday I continued to "yik" at him. (Why isn't that descriptive word in the dictionary?)

The following Monday, Kyle woke up out of sorts, but I was in better spirits. It reminded me of the newlyweds of yesteryear who had come up with the "perfect" solution. If he had a difficult day at the office, he returned home with the brim of his hat tipped back. If things hadn't been right for her, she turned up the corner of her apron. The stressful mate could then be comforted. But the day came—you guessed it—when he came in with the tipped brim *and* her apron corner was turned back!

"At least we're taking turns, dear," I told Kyle. "And I'll do my best to consider *your* feelings this week. I love you!"

ﾐ *TODAY'S DELIGHT:*
Comfort someone who is grieving. It may be a phone call, a letter, or perhaps red and pink roses.

Ready or Not, Here Comes Retirement!

I still vividly remember when my husband came home and announced he would retire early.

Suddenly I looked upon him as *old* and myself not far behind.

I'm not ready to go on the shelf! I thought. Who came up with this idea of retirement, anyway?

It started with Bismarck, a Prussian statesman, who recommended a small pension at age sixty-five. His advisers assured him that few people lived to that great age!

But there are many "greats" who did their best work between sixty-five and ninety.

> *Winston Churchill*—became prime minister of England at sixty-six, led his country through World War II, and remained active for another quarter of a century.
>
> *Golda Meir*—became prime minister of Israel at seventy one.
>
> *Albert Schweitzer*—was awarded the Nobel Peace Prize at seventy-seven and Great Britain's highest civilian award at ninety.
>
> *Grandma Moses*—started painting at seventy-six and sketched twenty-five pictures after her hundredth birthday.
>
> *Florence Nightingale*—a semi-invalid at

ninety-one, yet heads of government, authors, ministers, and politicians sought her advice.
John Wesley—preached, wrote, traveled at eighty-three—on horseback!

Now I don't feel so old!

&❧ *TODAY'S DELIGHT:*
Approaching retirement? Check with organizations that depend on volunteers. If you're not retired, consider giving a few hours to your church or the charity of your choice. Make a phone call today.

Hope for Your Future

*There is hope for your future, says the LORD: your
children shall come back to their own country.*

(Jeremiah 31:17 RSV)

I constantly agonize over my children's relationship
with the Lord. I ask him over and over, "When, Lord?
When will they return to their roots? When will they
begin serving you?"

The other morning the Lord and I engaged in a
dialogue (in my head).

"Lord, you said to train children in the right way,
and when they became old, they would not stray."
(See Proverbs 22:6.)

"But what is 'old'?" the Lord asked me.

I thought a moment. "When a child reaches an age
of accountability? Fifteen or sixteen?"

Silence.

"When he or she reaches twenty-one? Twenty-five?
(Pause) Thirty-five?"

Again silence.

"Lord, I want to see each of my children belong
wholly to you. Will I live that long? Is there any hope
for the future?"

"Do you trust me?" he gently asked.

"Oh yes! But Lord, look at their priorities! Material
possessions, sports, pursuing pleasure . . ."

"My timing is not your timing."

I had no answer, but my own words echoed in my
ears. *Is there any hope for the future?* Where had I read
that? Then I remembered Jeremiah 31:17. At some
long-ago date, I had written beside it in my Bible, "My
children will return to the Lord!" And they will—in
God's perfect timing!

PRAYER:
Be patient with me, Lord, as my loved ones find their
way back to their "own country."

ε▲ *TODAY'S DELIGHT:*
Read what God has to say about your children on the
next page.

Scriptures Pertaining to Your Children

"The fruit of your womb will be blessed."
(Deuteronomy 28:4 NIV)

"You have made the Lord your defender, the Most High your protector, and so no disaster will strike you, no violence will come near your home."
(Psalm 91:9-10 TEV)

"And you can also be very sure God will rescue the children of the godly." (Proverbs 11:21 TLB)

"I will pour out my Spirit on your offspring, and my blessing on your descendants." (Isaiah 44:3 NIV)

"I will contend with those who contend with you, and your children I will save." (Isaiah 49:25 NIV)

"All your children shall be taught by the LORD, and great shall be the prosperity of your children."
(Isaiah 54:13 NRSV)

"The work they do will be successful, and their children shall not meet with disaster. I will bless them and their descendants for all time to come."
(Isaiah 65:23-24 TEV)

"'So there is hope for your future,' declares the LORD. 'Your children will return to their own land.'"
(Jeremiah 31:17 NIV)

It also helps me to know that . . .

"His angels . . . do his bidding . . . obey his word . . . do his will."   (Psalm 103:20-21 NIV)

And what is his will?

"He longs for all to be saved"   (1 Timothy 2:4 TLB)

and

"is patient with you, not wanting anyone to perish, but everyone to come to repentance,"   (2 Peter 3:9 NIV)

and

"I, the Messiah, came to save the lost."
                    (Matthew 18:11 TLB)

The angels are also

"ministering spirits sent to serve those who will inherit salvation."   (Hebrews 1:14 NIV)

Jesus said:

"Let the little children come to me, and do not hinder them, for the kingdom of heaven belongs to such as these."   (Matthew 19:14 NIV)

He also promises

"the Holy Spirit . . . to each one of you who has been called by the Lord our God, and to your children"

(Acts 2:38-39 TLB)

and that

"a united family may, in God's plan, result in the children's salvation."   (1 Corinthians 7:14 TLB)

Socrates, indeed, when he was asked of what country he called himself, said, "Of the world"; for he considered himself an inhabitant and a citizen of the whole world.

—Cicero
(106–43 B.C.)

Delight in Travel

*You've seen the world—
The beauty and the wonder
and the power,
The shape of things, their
colors, lights and shades,
Changes, surprises—and God
made it all.*

—Robert Browning
(1812–1889), *Fra Lippo Lippi*

You Afraid?

We were preparing for takeoff when my elderly
  seatmate turned to me.
Smiling, she asked, "Are you frightened?"
"No," I replied.
"I always ask people in case I can help them overcome
  their fright."
She went on to explain, "I used to have an obsessive
  fear of flying. And, oh! the lovely trips I've denied
  myself!"
  She paused as if remembering those wasted years.
"Then my only son and his family moved across the
  country.
"Travel by bus or train wasted many precious days I
  could spend visiting.
"I *had* to do something!
"Then I discovered there is an emotion stronger than
  fear.
"Do you know what that is?"
Before I could reply, she said emphatically, "It's love!
"Love for my son, his wife, and those grandbabies was
  stronger than my fear of flying."
She flashed a sweet smile again.
"I'm eighty-four years old, but twice a year I fly five
  thousand miles, and I'm no longer afraid.
"I want others to experience freedom from the
  bondage of fear.

You Afraid?

"You know, the Good Book says, 'There is no fear in
     love, but perfect love casts out fear.'
"So I always ask my fellow passengers."
Satisfied that I was calm, and honest in my reply,
     she turned to the person on the other side of her.
"Sir, are you afraid?"

&— *TODAY'S DELIGHT:*
*Share with someone how God helped you conquer a fear
in your life. Or, turn a present fear over to him today.*

Freeway Travel

I could hardly believe it! We left Wheaton, Illinois, Friday at one o'clock in the afternoon, and were home in Walla Walla by Monday afternoon! Less than thirty-five driving hours! Interstate highways and cruise control made the miles fly by.

Oh, we took time to stop at rest areas, for meals, to sleep, and to take a few pictures, including bales of hay floating in a Nebraska field and flooded rivers around Ogden, Utah—both caused by late spring rains.

I remember long-distance treks of yesteryear. On one trip to California, we stopped in a Nevada town. In a city park, we feasted on homemade ice cream with fresh strawberries at an ice cream social. Such parks were great places to eat our packed lunches, let the kids expend pent-up energy on playground equipment, and stretch our legs. Sometimes we'd browse through Main Street shops. I still remember a pair of sandals I bought in an Indiana town.

Today's traveler is no longer charmed by small communities. Cultural differences are never apparent from interstate highways. Sometimes it's fun to bypass Howard Johnson restaurants along the Ohio or Pennsylvania turnpikes, for instance, and drive into a town. We did so at North Lima, Ohio, where I was fascinated by a family at the local Dairy Queen. The girls, about twelve and fifteen, wore quaint bonnets, as did their mother.

My writer's curiosity piqued, I walked up to their table.

"Are you folks Amish?" I asked.

"No, we're Mennonites."

I told the woman I'd written for a few Mennonite publications and was acquainted with some Mennonite people in the Portland, Oregon, area.

"They probably aren't as conservative as we are," she explained.

Such opportunities are lost in interstate traveling. But when you're in a hurry, the system is great. We faced a deadline, a granddaughter's high school graduation in Seattle, so we had no time to sightsee or soak up local color.

I believe we were the only drivers in the ten states through which we passed who observed the posted speed limits. But we didn't mind the hundreds of trucks zooming past. It was a far cry from being stuck behind a semi on a two-lane twisting highway.

Someday, however, I'd like to travel those back roads at a leisurely pace and experience the real heart of America.

&❧ *TODAY'S DELIGHT:*
Discover the charm of a small town. Perhaps next weekend you can visit one in your area.

I Spy—a Sign!

Whether traveling in the country or city, I enjoy the scenery. In the city, you might ask? Yes! The scenery of inspirational signs. Church signboards are the most likely places to look for these words of wisdom. But what a joy to see them elsewhere, as proprietors share their faith with the public. I've spotted the following signs on business establishments:

At a dry cleaners:
> *Bible dusty?*
> *Heart rusty!*

At a chiropractic clinic:
> *We cannot direct the wind,*
> *but we can adjust the sail.*

At a grocery store:
> *God gives us the ingredients for our daily bread,*
> *but he expects us to do the baking.*

At an auto parts lot:
> *A Bible that's falling apart*
> *Usually belongs to a person who isn't.*

At a funeral chapel:
> *Nobody ever got hurt cutting corners on a square deal.*

I Spy—a Sign!

Church signboards in my area have offered these words:

At an Assembly of God church:
C H -- C H
What's missing?
U R

At a Baptist church:
This church is not a club for saints,
but a hospital for sinners.

At a Nazarene church:
The Bible is the only book whose author
is always present when it is read.

My eyes were drawn to these out-of-town church signs:

In Portland, Oregon:
If you have an unpleasant neighbor,
chances are he does too.

In Santa Rosa, California:
A good neighbor doubles the value of a house.

In Columbiana, Ohio:
Praise! Letting off esteem!

In Selma, Alabama:
Many people grow small by trying to be big.

In North Jacksonville, Florida:
Taking applications for heaven. Apply within.

Next time you travel, be on the lookout for inspiration in both likely and unlikely places.

&❧ *TODAY'S DELIGHT:*
Be alert to uplifting signs in your "neck of the woods."

A Southern Washington

Doris Martin was a delightful tour guide. Few people came to tour the Washington Wilkes Historical Museum in November, so we received undivided attention.

The museum is located in an antebellum ("before the Civil War") house in Washington, Georgia.

When we travel and speak of our state, we are often mistaken for residents of the nation's capital. But mention "Washington" in the east-central section of Georgia, and folks assume you mean the original place named after America's first president. In fact, he was honored, not as president, but as a great American general when Washington, Georgia, was incorporated January 23, 1870.

We were impressed with Doris's knowledge of local and state history as she showed us relics from "The War between the States." That's how most Southerners refer to the Civil War.

She proudly pointed out Jefferson Davis's war chest. English sympathizers had presented it to the Confederate president. The United Daughters of the Confederacy purchased the war chest from Mrs. Bell Virgin, daughter of a Confederate officer, Colonel John Weems. He was given the chest by a member of Davis's staff.

Apparently a man from the North offered to buy the war chest for one thousand dollars. Mrs. Virgin refused. The story goes he ran his bid to three thousand dollars, a huge sum in those days. Newspapers printed the account, saying, "The Unwise Virgin told him she wouldn't sell the relic at any price to a man who's been an enemy of the South." A Pittsburgh man read about the incident and was so impressed with her loyalty, he requested her hand in marriage. One can safely assume she turned him down.

I found my maiden name to be prominent in Washington, Georgia. In fact, a man named Edward Pope was mayor at the time. I purchased note cards bearing a sketch of yet another antebellum mansion, the Pembroke Pope House.

We lunched at "Another Thyme," a unique restaurant in the lobby of the old Fitzpatrick Hotel. I ordered the soup of the day, chicken and water chestnut. Delicious!

As in many Southern towns, the square is dominated by a memorial to men who died during the Civil War. In Washington, Georgia, the statue overlooked a lovingly tended patch of blooming cotton.

We knew we were in the South!

&~ *TODAY'S DELIGHT:*
Check out a library book about a section of our country with which you are unfamiliar. Discover that we are truly the UNITED States of America.

Mini-Miracle Trip

Oh, what parents do for their kids! I thought, as I wrapped the crystal cake tray in tissue paper and towels.

How could I find any delight in this "duty" trip? I'd barely recuperated from our daughter's wedding a month before. Shower and wedding gifts, still displayed on the card table, spilled over onto TV trays in the corner of the living room. I carefully prepared each gift for the twenty-six-hundred-mile trip. We planned to place breakables in Laurie's Chevy Citation, which still held enough rice to feed the neighborhood! The car would then be positioned in the center of a twenty-two-foot truck, with furniture arranged around it.

What relief to get chairs, lamps, water bed, and other household goods out of our crowded basement, where they'd been stored since arriving from overseas.

Laurie met her future husband while teaching school on an American military post in Germany. After his discharge, J.T. found employment in the South, just two months prior to the wedding date.

He arrived in town at three o'clock on Friday afternoon, and the wedding took place Saturday afternoon. The bridal couple flew back to Georgia at 5:30 in the morning on Sunday. We volunteered to drive a rented truck with all her belongings to their new home.

Prior to our November departure date, I began to worry. *What if we get caught in a blizzard? What if china and crystal are broken? What if we can't handle that big truck?*

Then the trip began, each day giving us a mini-miracle.

DAY 1

We needed only to put suitcases in the truck when we discovered the padlock key was missing. We looked in the truck cab, turned over leaves and weeds between the house and the parked truck—no key. We stopped our frantic searching long enough to pray, then retraced our steps. How could that key be lying on the cab floor in plain sight?

DAY 2

Twenty miles from Ogden, Utah, the gas gauge suddenly registered empty. The truck coughed and sputtered as we coasted up to the gas pumps at the first station off the freeway.

DAY 3

We awakened to Wyoming's first snowfall in Rawlins, four inches with near zero visibility. Before leaving the motel room, I opened a Gideon Bible and read in Psalm 84:7, "They go from strength to strength. . . ." For one hundred miles, as semis jackknifed on the highway, I repeated "strength to strength" until the snow turned to rain.

DAY 4
The welcome rain changed to a solid sheet of ice during the night at Goodland, Kansas. Through wind and sleet, we continued to ask the Lord for "strength to strength." Late that evening, "Aunt" Manila welcomed us to her tiny mobile home. Mutual friends had told her of our trip. She'd written them, "My place is two miles off the interstate. Tell the Waites to stop here." Despite the use of a walker, she offered us a comfortable bed, delicious breakfast, and prayers for our safe journey.

DAY 5
Weariness overcame us as we drove through St. Louis, a corner of Illinois, and into Kentucky, headed for Franklin, where cousins lived. What a winding route in the blackest night! Our safe arrival became that day's mini-miracle.

DAY 6
The Tennessee mountain pass in blinding rain wasn't half as frightening as 4:00 P.M. Atlanta traffic. Cars weaved in and out. Each time we slammed on the brakes, I fully expected the Chevy to join us in the cab.

Athens at last! As we turned into the shopping mall to meet our daughter, a driver abruptly cut in front, and we avoided a crash by inches!

But we'd made it! A week later, highways we'd traveled were closed with six- to eight-foot snowdrifts!

We'd gone from "strength to strength," and God

made us aware that each day brought a miracle from his hand!

🐚 *TODAY'S DELIGHT:*
Contact someone who is planning a trip. Tell your friend you will pray for his or her safe journey. In your own life, look for a mini-miracle from God today.

It's What's Inside That Counts

If a man comes into your church dressed in
expensive clothes and with valuable gold rings on
his fingers, and at the same moment another man
comes in who is poor and dressed in threadbare
clothes, and you make a lot of fuss over the rich
man and give him the best seat in the house and
say to the poor man, "You can stand over there if
you like, or else sit on the floor"—well, judging a
man by his wealth shows that you are guided by
wrong motives.   (James 2:2-4 TLB)

We'd been traveling in the British Isles for almost
three weeks. The little rented Ford Escort had
become our close friend as we maneuvered it down
narrow roads, constantly reminding ourselves, "Left
side! Left side!"

"What day is this?" I asked my husband. He
glanced at his watch.

"Sunday." He paused, and with emphasis, added, "A
sun day!" We'd been so deluged with rain the few days
before that we hadn't even caught a glimpse of Loch
Lomond. But today the sun was shining brightly.

I was about to say how I missed attending church
services, when we rounded a corner and there at the
top of a hill, stood a small church.[1]

"I think that church is about to begin. Let's go!"

50

My husband was less than enthusiastic. "Look at us. We're not dressed properly. Besides, it's almost 11:30."

But people were headed toward the church. Seeing my glint of determination, he found a parking spot.

As we trudged up the hill, I mentally rehearsed how to explain our appearance. Sure enough, there was a greeter at the door. I mumbled something about being travelers.

"Ah, Lass, the good Lord dain't care how ye are dressed!"

How grateful I was for that! As I listened to the delightful sermon on Colossians 1:27, "Christ in You, the Hope of Glory," and participated in Holy Communion, I had the assurance that it's what's inside that counts.

That brief hour set the tone for the rest of the day as we left the tiny church refreshed, renewed, and ready to continue on toward Edinburgh.

PRAYER:
Father, help me to extend a hand of friendship to anyone coming into my church, and never to judge by appearances.

---

[1]We learned that the Kenmore Church of Scotland had a rich history dating bacvk to 1579, when the first church was built. The building assumed its present form when it was reconstructed by the third earl of Breadalbane in 1760. People were walking up the slope.

It's What's Inside That Counts

&❧ *TODAY'S DELIGHT:*
Visit another church—either in your community or
when you are traveling in an unfamiliar area.

Dutch Treat

The rain began in earnest just as my husband, daughter, and I left the Nijmegen train station and tried to locate the tourist information office. By the time we found refuge under a canopy, we were soaked. Pulling out our trusty Berlitz Dutch Guidebook, we communicated with a young man who said, "Closed."

What to do? On foot and carrying suitcases in a strange country at six o'clock in the evening, we felt helpless. The rain subsided and the crowd under the shelter dispersed. Language barrier or not, we had to find lodging.

Making our way down the street, it started pouring again. As we dodged in and out of doorways, we spied a sign, "Larry's—English spoken." We hadn't had supper, so we decided to eat and dry out there.

"May I help you?" a waitress asked. She explained that English was her second language because her father worked for an international corporation. What a relief to explain our plight to someone who understood! She asked what we could afford for lodging, then offered to check with the nearby hotels. After serving our meal, she got on the phone, and soon returned with a slip of paper. "Hotel Europa—Bloemerstraat 65." She had also written a note to the proprietor and drawn us a map. I shall long remember

Annemaria Couwenberg, the waitress at "Larry's," Molenstraat 99, Nijmegen, Holland.

Nor shall I soon forget another Dutch woman. We were trying to get to Overloon, about eight miles from Venray where we got off the train. We wanted to visit the War Museum and Peace Chapel, the site of the fiercest tank battle of World War II.

A woman overheard our conversation with the trainmaster, who was trying to explain that the next bus would not leave for two hours.

"Overloon?" she asked. We nodded. Gesturing toward her car, she indicated she would give us a lift. With the help of our guidebook, we found out where she lived. Checking the map later, we realized how far she had driven out of her way to help three American tourists.

I truly fell in love with the gracious Dutch people!

❧ TODAY'S DELIGHT:
The next time you encounter someone who is lost or in need of assistance, go the extra mile to help him or her.

Come Celebrate Together

Make every effort to live in peace with all men.

(Hebrews 12:14 NIV)

Toward evening we drove into one of the smallest countries in the world. Liechtenstein, which lies between Switzerland and Austria, covers only sixty-one square miles, six square miles *less* than Washington, D.C.!

We checked into a Vaduz hotel, picturesquely perched on a hillside in this capital city. In the valley below, a carnival was in progress. To the left of our balcony, the royal palace glittered with hundreds of lights.

Suddenly fireworks illumined the surrounding mountains. Curious, we checked with the hotel clerk. He explained it was Switzerland's Independence Day, and, as was the custom, his countrymen joined their neighbors in celebrating this special occasion.

How wonderful, I thought, if more nations joined other countries in their commemoration of cultural or historical events. What a great way to promote understanding among peoples!

Come to think of it, communities can do that too. Each year, Hispanics in our area celebrate Cinco de Mayo (Fifth of May) honoring the Mexican Army's 1862 victory over an invading French force. Perhaps I can join my neighbors at this year's Cinco de Mayo festival.

PRAYER:
Lord, open my eyes, ears, and heart to people who are from different cultural and ethnic backgrounds. Amen.

🕊 *TODAY'S DELIGHT:*
Celebrate an ethnic event, either in your own
community or in one nearby.

Forgiving Is a Delight

*Be gentle and ready to forgive; never hold grudges.
Remember, the Lord forgave you, so you must
forgive others.* (Colossians 3:13 TLB)

We were visiting the medieval walled city of
Rothenburg. After marveling at ancient buildings and
artifacts, we spied a more modern monument. With
our limited German, we tried to read the sign.

A German man standing beside us translated: "We
believe in our borders and in a free Germany." He
scrutinized us for a moment. Feeling uncomfortable,
we began to turn away. He added scornfully, "It's a
memorial to the men killed in World Wars I and II."

Later, my husband, daughter, and I discussed the
episode. Had the German man carried bitterness
since the forties? Was he a soldier then? Had his
father or perhaps a brother been killed fighting for
their homeland? Did he still look upon Americans as
the "enemy"?

How sad, I thought. Then I squirmed a bit. I may
have no trouble with national forgiveness. But I
remember a man who once robbed my husband of a
job. I disliked him for years. What about the neighbor
who spread gossip about one of my children? Or the
relative who treated me so shabbily? Do I continue to
harbor grudges?

PRAYER:
Father, help me to be gentle and ready to forgive.
Cleanse me of any hostile feelings that block your
love.

❧ *TODAY'S DELIGHT:*
Ask God to reveal the source of any hidden hurt and
help you to forgive.

"Guh-dye, Mite!"

"See the shape!" the tour bus driver announced. We looked out the windows but couldn't see any round, oblong, or odd-shaped sight. Then he pointed, "See—the shape on the hill over there!"

Oh, *sheep!* We all laughed at our inability to translate the driver's Australian accent into more understandable "American" English.

Even after deciphering the accent, we heard strange terms such as:

> *Fair dinkum*—when something is great or fantastic
> *Chinwag*—talking
> *Chooks*—large chickens (younger ones are still *chicks*)
> *Plain wrappers*—unmarked police cars

And my favorite:

Pull up—when someone is bugging you

During the remainder of the tour, difficult passengers were occasionally told to "Pull up," in a nonthreatening tone of voice, of course. It worked much better than "Get lost!" "Bug off!" or "Chill out!" especially when accompanied by a smile.

Our words are important, but the manner in which

they're said can make a great deal of difference in the results.

Our kids used to experiment with the dog. "You're a stupid mutt! Get out of here!" they'd say in a soft, lilting voice, which brought forth a joyous tail-wagging.

"I think you're a great pet!" they'd utter in an angry, loud voice. The dog would cower and sneak off into a corner.

We should strive for the perfect combination—kind words expressed in a kind manner.

 ☙ *TODAY'S DELIGHT:*
Use loving tones in your speech. If you slip, don't despair. Start anew tomorrow morning.

Hospitality par Excellence

Love as brethren . . . be courteous. (1 Peter 3:8)

While visiting in our Japanese sister city, Sasayama, we asked the local travel agent to arrange a trip to Hiroshima. That evening he called our host family with the message that someone would meet us at the Hiroshima train station. We couldn't afford a tour guide, so we planned to find our own way around. We tried to explain this to our host, but he kept pointing to the word *niece* in the dictionary.

When we arrived in Hiroshima, we began to look for a taxi stand. Suddenly a young woman breathlessly approached us. "A thousand pardons, Mr. and Mrs. Waite. I went to the wrong platform.

"I am Noriko, niece of Mr. Yamauti, Sasayama travel agent. I desire to show you my city. Perhaps I may also learn to speak English better."

Noriko insisted on paying for the taxi to the hotel, where she had left her bicycle. She accompanied us to dinner and the next morning took us to the Peace Museum and surrounding area. We discovered she had taken the day off work to serve as our guide. Upon our departure, she accompanied us to the station, handing us a lovely gift as we boarded.

I live in a small farming community. How can *I* show such warm hospitality to foreign visitors?

Hmmm . . . there *are* exchange students attending college here. What a good place to start!

PRAYER:
Lord, give me courage to reach out to people who may not speak my language or who may be different from me. Amen.

• *TODAY'S DELIGHT:*
Check with an area college for the names of foreign students. Invite them into your home for a visit and/or dinner.

Watch Your Tongue!

Do not let any unwholesome talk come out of your mouths, but only what is helpful for building others up according to their needs, that it may benefit those who listen.

(Ephesians 4:29 NIV)

We watched the Maori concert group with fascination—the women in their woven flax skirts as they twirled poi balls—the men with painted faces performing a war dance. The audience roared with delight as the men stuck out their tongues.

Later at the Whakarewarewa Cultural Center in Rotorua, a Maori guide told us, "The most respected Maori warriors were the ugliest. The protruding tongue added to their fierce appearance. It was a sign of defiance meant to intimidate the enemy." When someone in the tour group snickered, she added, "What does a child sometimes do after he is disciplined? When Mom's back is turned, he sticks his tongue out at her."

I'm more apt to give my "enemy" a tongue-*lashing!* But the Bible has several better suggestions. One is in the above Ephesians passage. The Old Testament says much the same in Proverbs 12:18: "Reckless words pierce like a sword, but the tongue of the wise brings healing" (NIV).

I must choose to speak words of healing, words that

benefit the listener; otherwise, I'd better keep my tongue quiet!

PRAYER:
Father, the next time I face an unpleasant situation or person, please help me to utter words of encouragement and love.

2ª TODAY'S DELIGHT:
Make an effort to wear a "delight-filled" facial expression all day.

A Traveler's Guide to Heaven

Accommodations
Arrangements for first-class accommodations have been made in advance.

In my Father's house are many mansions. . . . I go to prepare a place for you.   (John 14:2)

Passports
Persons seeking entry will not be permitted past the gates without having proper credentials and having their names registered with the ruling Authority.

There shall in no wise enter into it any thing that defileth . . . but they which are written in the Lamb's book of life.   (Revelation 21:27)

Departure Times
The exact date of departure has not been announced. Travelers are advised to be prepared to leave at short notice.

It is not for you to know the times or the seasons, which the Father hath put in his own power.   (Acts 1:7)

Tickets
Your ticket is a written pledge that guarantees your journey. It should be claimed and its promises kept firmly in hand.

He that heareth my word, and believeth on him that sent me, hath everlasting life, and shall not come into condemnation; but is passed from death unto life.

(John 5:24)

Customs
Only one declaration is required while going through customs.

I declare unto you the gospel. . . . that Christ died for our sins according to the Scriptures; and that he was buried, and that he rose again the third day.

(1 Corinthians 15:1, 3-4)

Immigration
All passengers are classified as immigrants, since they are taking up permanent residence in a new country. The quota is unlimited.

They desire a better country, that is, a heavenly . . . for he hath prepared for them a city.   (Hebrews 11:16)

Luggage
No luggage whatsoever can be taken.

We brought nothing into this world, and it is certain we can carry nothing out.   (1 Timothy 6:7)

Air Passage
Travelers going directly by air are advised to watch daily for indications of imminent departure.

We which are alive and remain shall be caught up
together with them in the clouds, to meet the Lord in
the air: and so shall we ever be with the Lord.

(1 Thessalonians 4:17)

Vaccination and Inoculation
Injections are not needed, as diseases are unknown at
the destination.

God shall wipe away all tears from their eyes; and
there shall be no more death, neither sorrow, nor
crying, neither shall there be any more pain.

(Revelation 21:4)

Currency
Supplies of currency may be forwarded ahead to await
the passenger's arrival. Deposits should be as large as
possible.

Lay up for yourselves treasures in heaven, where
neither moth nor rust doth corrupt, and where
thieves do not break through nor steal.   (Matthew 6:20)

Clothing
A complete and appropriate new wardrobe is provided
for each traveler.

He hath clothed me with the garments of salvation, he
hath covered me with the robe of righteousness.

(Isaiah 61:10)

Time Changes

Resetting of watches will not be necessary—nor will the watches.

The city had no need of the sun, neither of the moon, to shine in it: for the glory of God did lighten it, and the Lamb is the light thereof. And . . . there shall be no night there. (Revelation 21:23-25)

Reservations

Booking is now open. Apply at once.

Now is the accepted time; behold, now is the day of salvation. (2 Corinthians 6:2)

Coronation Ceremony

The highlight of the journey is the welcoming reception and coronation, which await each new arrival.

There is laid up for me a crown of righteousness, which the Lord, the righteous judge, shall give me at that day: and not to me only, but unto all them also that love his appearing. (2 Timothy 4:8)

This brochure by Mrs. Marcelle Price was also reprinted in *Decision,* August 1968, 7.

Saints are persons who make it easier for others to believe in God.

—Nathan
Soderblom
(1866–1931)

Precious in the sight of the LORD is the death of his saints.

—Psalm 116:15

Delight in Everyday Saints

Be it resolved:
The earth is the Lord's
and the fullness thereof.

Be it resolved:
That the fullness thereof
belongs to the saints.

Be it resolved:
That we are the saints!

*—Document found in
old New England church*

Champion of the Homeless

Less than ten years ago, Gary was the typical Yuppie, a dental salesman winning national awards and moving all over the country. He was married by the time he was twenty-one and divorced by twenty-seven. A bizarre set of circumstances changed his life forever.

It started with a series of arguments Gary had with a dentist friend about life's origin. He began to read voraciously, including the Bible.

"I remember the exact instant I became a Christian. It was March 22 at 3:15 P.M. on a beach in Venice, Florida," he recalls. "I stood there looking out at the horizon, talking to God."

Two other seemingly unrelated events took place—a TV show on poverty that left him visibly shaken, and a fishing trip in the Florida Keys. There he met a man who sold dental supplies in Gary's hometown in the Northwest. The two switched areas. Shortly thereafter, Gary was laid off, and started going to college with a goal of becoming a missionary in some Third World country.

By this time, Gary had married a former high school friend whose parents were strong Christians. Learning of his heart for the poor, Gary's mother-in-law suggested he volunteer at the local Christian Aid Center.

The director was approaching retirement and told Gary he'd been praying for a replacement. But Gary had his sights set on working overseas. However, within a few weeks, he knew he was where God wanted him. Besides the ongoing demands of the center, Gary has been indefatigable in the establishment of a house for homeless and abused women and children. God's latest nudge has prompted Gary to solicit the community's help in starting a boarding school for troubled and homeless teens.

Recently Gary and his wife *did* have the opportunity to serve briefly in a poor country when they spent two weeks in the slums of Tijuana, Mexico. Gary was especially touched by an orphan named David and recalls that special moment when he hugged the blind child: "He leaned against my hand as I stroked his face. I felt a bizarre sense of peace, as though the world was standing still. There was only David and me. The words of Jesus came to life in my heart—words I'd experienced so many times before, but now in a new and marvelous way—'What you do for the least of these, you do for me.' At the risk of sounding crazy, I felt in a very special way that I was holding Jesus in my arms."

There are many everyday saints like Gary who show God's love to the troubled, the homeless, and the poor at home and abroad. The rest of us hold you in high regard and thank the Lord for your servant hearts.

❧ *TODAY'S DELIGHT:*
Write a note of appreciation to someone who works with the homeless in your community. Or check with your local Christian Aid Center (Rescue Mission) about their current needs (food, clothing, etc.) and help supply those items.

She Did What She Could

She was a small child when her eyes began to trouble her. Her parents took her to a doctor who inadvertently used the wrong treatment. Later she was taken to a New York specialist who told the distraught mother that surgery would do nothing. As a result, the child was blind the rest of her life. She lived for almost ninety years in total darkness, yet during that time composed over eight thousand hymns!

As I checked through several hymnals, I was struck with the many times Fanny Crosby's songs spoke of sight and light. You may be familiar with some of them:

> *Perfect submission, perfect delight,*
> *Visions of rapture now burst on my sight. . . .*
> —"Blessed Assurance, Jesus Is Mine"

> *Gushing from the rock before me,*
> *Lo! a spring of joy I see. . . .*
> —"All the Way My Savior Leads Me"

> *He hideth my soul in the cleft of the rock,*
> *Where rivers of pleasures I see.*
> —"He Hideth My Soul"

How often Fanny's hymns expressed confidence that she would see her Lord face to face:

> *But purer and higher, and greater will be*
> *Our wonder, our transport, when Jesus we see.*
> —"To God Be the Glory"

74

Trusting only in thy merit,
Would I seek thy face. . . .
—"Pass Me Not, O Gentle Savior"

Oh, the soul-thrilling rapture
 when I view his blessed face,
And the luster of His kindly beaming eye. . . .
—"My Savior First of All"

How many times during those ninety years must Fanny Crosby have felt despair! Braille was not as widely accepted as it is today. There were no tape libraries with talking books, no Seeing-Eye dogs. Yet, when asked if she ever felt bitterness toward the doctor, she replied, "No. It may have been a mistake on the doctor's part, but not on God's part."

This everyday saint's gravestone contains a quotation that a casual observer might miss. It was spoken by Christ after Mary anointed him with an expensive perfume. Some objected to this "waste," but Jesus said, "She did what she could."

 🐦 *TODAY'S DELIGHT:*
Read or sing all of the verses in one or more of the above hymns, or read one of the many biographies that have been written about the amazing Fanny Crosby. Or consider getting involved in a program for the blind. (I once read several chapters from a textbook onto a cassette tape for a blind college student.)

Narcissa Whitman
—Saint at Waiilatpu

The view from my dining room window is a changing panorama—snow-covered peaks in the winter, lush shades of green in the summer. It is the same view that greeted Narcissa Whitman day after day from her mission home at Waiilatpu, six miles west of present-day Walla Walla, Washington.

She was only eleven when she made a public confession of faith. By the time she was sixteen, she felt a call from God to serve as a missionary. But single women were not accepted by mission boards. The call grew stronger when, in an 1833 issue of *The Christian Advocate,* she read about four Nez Percé braves who journeyed East seeking the "white man's Book of Heaven."

Then she met Marcus Whitman, whose desire to serve in Oregon Territory matched hers. After a brief courtship, Narcissa Prentiss married Dr. Whitman on February 18, 1836. After ten arduous months of travel from New York State, they arrived at Waiilatpu in the Walla Walla Valley. The following March, their daughter, Alice Clarissa, was born on her mother's twenty-ninth birthday. Her birth lessened the animosity among the Cayuse Indians whom the Whitmans hoped to Christianize.

One Sunday afternoon in June, 1839, while her parents were engrossed in reading, Alice Clarissa took

two cups to "get water for supper" from the nearby
Walla Walla River. When they found Alice's little body,
Narcissa cried out, "She is not mine, but thine. She
has only been lent to me for a little season, and now,
dearest Savior, thou hast the best right to her."

After her daughter's death, Narcissa immersed
herself with new determination into the slow and
discouraging task of teaching the Cayuse children
about God, taking in any child needing a home. At one
time, she mothered a brood of eleven youngsters—
two half-Indian daughters of mountain men Jim
Bridger and Joe Meek; an abandoned Indian boy;
Marcus's nephew; and the seven Sager youngsters
whose parents had died coming West. She also welcomed and helped the families staying at the emigrant
house, an additional facility built to accommodate
travelers.

In the meantime, Marcus provided medical care to
white men and Indians alike. Conditions at Indian
camps appalled him, and he confided to Narcissa,
"There's so much starvation among the Indians,
besides their tribal wars. How we must hasten to
teach them of Christ's salvation so they can face death
without fear! They must be shown the love of God.
Until the Indians kill us or drive us out, we shall stay
and work."

His words proved to be prophetic. In November
1847, a measles epidemic swept through both Indian
and white settlements, but the red man had no
immunity to the disease. Cayuse troublemakers

convinced the tribe that Dr. Whitman was poisoning them. On November 29, these braves broke into the mission house, killing the Whitmans and seven others. By the week's end, fourteen people were dead.

Today Narcissa and her husband remain symbols of the resolute missionary spirit that led to the settlement and spread of Christianity in the Pacific Northwest.

≈ *TODAY'S DELIGHT:*
Check out a book about the Whitmans, or a missionary of your choice, from your church or public library. Delight in how these everyday saints have served the Lord around the world.

Disarming Love

Love is patient, love is kind. . . . Love does not delight in evil but rejoices in the truth.

(1 Corinthians 13:4, 6 NIV)

Virginia Randolph was a pioneer in black education. She began teaching in a southern rural school in 1892. As she tried to instill high ethical standards along with the "Three *R*s," many parents resented it.

In fact, one mother bragged about whipping every teacher at that school. She vowed Miss Randolph would be next.

One day, Virginia saw the woman standing on the porch with a long stick. She'd just finished reading 1 Corinthians 13 to her class.

"Children," she began, keeping her voice steady, "this morning I'm going to pray, 'Lord, have mercy on the dear mother that came to school.' So glad to see you, dear mother." Virginia then led the boys and girls in singing, "I Need Thee Every Hour."

She continued, "Now, students, this has been the first mother to visit school. She has two lovely children, and you know the hand that rocks the cradle rules the world. Don't you feel proud? I'll ask her to speak to us."

That mother was so touched, her eyes filled with tears.

"I came for one thing and found another," she said.

"I will never disturb the classroom again." She kept her promise and became a willing school worker.

Isn't it amazing how love disarms hostility? It was true in 1892 and is just as true one hundred years later.

PRAYER:
Father, help me to look at the unlovely of the world through eyes of love—your eyes.

❧ *TODAY'S DELIGHT:*
Volunteer at a local school—to read during library hour, supervise in the cafeteria or on the playground, or ask a teacher how you can help on a one-time basis.

God's Jewel

Her life hasn't been easy.
Helen's only son, adopted as an infant, is mentally
   impaired.
Her husband died in a tragic home accident.
But Helen is one of the most joyous Christians I've
   ever known.
She teaches illiterates to read.
She has driven folks from her Indiana home to the
   Mayo Clinic in Minnesota, and a friend to Arkansas
   to visit her family.
She works faithfully in her church.
Helen rarely talks about her sparse income, her
   health problems, or what the future holds.
She is truly a saint in God's kingdom of light
   (Colossians 1:12) and one of heaven's jewels.

Lord, when trouble comes, how I gripe, grumble,
   fuss, and fume!
I complain, "Nobody knows the trouble I've seen," but
   I forget the "Glory, hallelujah!"
Take the hardships of my life and, like diamond dust,
   use them to polish me so that I may become a jewel
   like Helen.

ぅ *TODAY'S DELIGHT:*
Contact one of "God's jewels" in your life, and thank
him or her for being a friend.

He Served to the End

The diagnosis did not stop him. The uncertainty of
the future did not stop him. The pain did not stop him.
He refused to give up. So citizens who did not know
him personally were not prepared. Nor perhaps were
the members of the city council when they read his
letter at their meeting.

> I have enjoyed very much the twenty-one-plus
> years I have served on this council, two of which
> as mayor. . . . My best wishes to my fellow
> council members and to the citizens of Walla
> Walla as this fine city continues to grow and
> prosper.

Three days later, Dan Swank lost the battle with his
enemy—cancer. But Dan would be the first to tell
folks not to spend time grieving—but to use that
energy getting involved in worthwhile activities.

His obituary, along with page-one articles in the
local paper, read like "Mr. Who's Who in Small Town
America." Dan served on the hospital and Red Cross
boards as well as the park commission and chaired
the United Fund and Boy Scout Fund (although he
had only two daughters). With his daughters' inter-
ests in mind, he took his stint as a PTA president both
on the elementary and junior high levels. Numerous
other organizations benefited from Dan's leadership,

as did his beloved church, where he served in many capacities, including church treasurer and head usher.

Throughout his illness, Dan continued to head one of the ushering teams under my husband's leadership. Others would have given up much sooner, but not Dan. Then came Saturday evenings when Dan phoned, apologetically suggesting a substitute, and finally he called, asking to be removed from the usher list. He could no longer stand for that length of time.

But he could sit—sit at council meetings, helping to chart the future of his community. His main goal was "to make Walla Walla a city that the citizens are proud of—a beautiful city, a safe city, and one they would be proud to show to anyone who comes to town."

There are Dan Swanks all over this wonderful country of ours—unsung heroes working in schools, communities, and churches. They are truly everyday saints.

> *TODAY'S DELIGHT:*
> *Write a letter to a city, school, or church official. Tell him or her how proud you are to have your family represented by such a loyal public servant.*

Grandpa's Gift

A good man leaves an inheritance for his children's children. (Proverbs 13:22 NIV)

My husband's brother died recently.
We wondered how his children were faring.
We learned that one of his colleagues had been
    helping Joni through her dad's illness and death.
In fact, he led her to the Lord!
As Joni shared her new life with me, she said,
"When I was a little girl, Grandpa gave me a Bible.
"That was the beginning.
"When I began to deal with Dad's illness, I turned to
    Grandpa's gift.
"It took twenty years for the results!"
I wasn't surprised that Grandpa planted seeds in the
    life of his granddaughter.
This godly man did the same for his
    daughter-in-law—me!

Lord, I have grandchildren of my own now.
How can I contribute to their spiritual growth?
Show me ways in which I can leave a godly
    inheritance for my children's children.

❧ TODAY'S DELIGHT:
Consider giving a Bible or a portion of the Scriptures to
someone.

In Prison, and You Visited Me

Frances Scott felt the Lord's presence every time the clanging doors closed behind her. She loved her work at the prison—playing for Sunday services, visiting on the other days. She felt privileged to do small favors, contact relatives, or make phone calls for the inmates. She became a special friend to several prison wives who contacted her when there was nobody else to listen.

During those years, the prison chaplain said of Frances, "The Lord is using her in a beautiful way. I especially appreciate her knowledge of the Scriptures, her awareness of what really works in changing the lives of inmates, and her willingness to devote time to the prison ministry."

That commitment was put to the supreme test one day about twelve years ago, when Frances was in her seventies. An inmate friend on work release came to her door one morning. He said his car was broken down and he needed a ride to work. Frances didn't hesitate one moment.

As she was about to get into her car, the man said, "I'm sorry, Mrs. Scott, but I have to tie you up."

Frances's heart raced but she answered, "You don't have to do that. I'll take you wherever you want to go."

Thus began an eleven-hour drive across the state. Frances prayed and then began witnessing to the man.

"You can begin a new life right now, if you'll say yes to Jesus," she told him.

Several times during the ordeal, Frances was sure he'd turn the car around. When they reached a certain city, he sent Frances for food. Before she could summon help, the man had disappeared.

He was apprehended the next morning and later sentenced on charges of escape and abduction.

"I was never afraid for a minute," Frances said. "I just visualized Jesus sitting in the back seat."

She sent him a copy of *The Living Bible,* and within a short time the man committed his life to Christ.

I'll never forget what Charles Colson, founder of Prison Fellowship, said about my friend: "Frances is a caring Christian willing to show the 'tough love' Jesus asks for and willing to pay the cost to be a true follower. One hundred more like her across the country, and we'd have a mighty reformation."

Frances now lives in another city closer to her son. But this everyday saint still ministers to others in her retirement complex.

  TODAY'S DELIGHT:
Visit someone in your local jail or in an area nursing home. Or write, call, or visit someone who is "imprisoned" by circumstances—perhaps a shut-in or a friend facing difficult days.

A Latecomer to the Harvest

The call came late on a Tuesday afternoon. Dad was
sinking fast! I'd better come to Michigan soon. I had
to make travel arrangements and then meet with a
college class to schedule the rest of the quarter. All
day Wednesday I wondered, *Will I be in time?* Friends
prayed specifically for God's perfect timing.

I arrived at Metro Airport Thursday night. Was I
too late?

"We almost lost Dad yesterday," my brother said.
"But I kept telling him you were coming."

As I entered the hospital room, Dad whispered,
"I've been waiting for you, Shirl!"

The next morning the doctor confided, "Frankly, I
didn't expect to see your father today. You must have
brought good medicine from the West."

Dad rallied. Although critically ill, he was lucid, and
I stayed by his side the next four days. I could hardly
bear to watch him suffer and cried for God to take
him.

I slept at my brother's home Sunday night and was
awakened suddenly during the early hours that
Monday morning. Had I heard a voice? Perhaps not,
but a strong impression.

"Your dad isn't ready yet."

"Is that you, Lord?" Silence.

As soon as I got to the hospital, I gently approached
my father. He confessed his sins and accepted Jesus

Christ as his Savior. Father and daughter shared a special prayer, and I knew Dad had become one of God's saints.

But what if he lingered? Should I stay, despite obligations at home? If I left, would I face a return trip?

I sat next to Dad's bedside and wrote a poem as the early afternoon sun streamed through the hospital window. A dozen or so verses poured from my pen, some to my earthly father, and others to my heavenly Father. (See the following page.)

Late that afternoon, Dad stepped into that glorious pain-free eternal life with his God. The funeral was on Thursday; I came home on my scheduled flight Friday.

God's timing was perfect!

≈ *TODAY'S DELIGHT:*
Read the parable of the workers in the harvest (Matthew 20:1-16). The footnote in my Life Application Bible *(NRSV) says, "This parable is not about rewards but about salvation. It is a strong teaching about grace, God's generosity. We shouldn't begrudge those who turn to God in the last moments of life because, in reality, no one deserves eternal life."*

Dad's Poem

(Written about three o'clock on the Monday afternoon
of Dad's entry into heaven)

Take my dad, O Holy One.
Take my dad today.
Take my dad, O Holy One.
Take him now, I pray.

O Lord and precious Savior,
I know it's not thy will
For him to live and suffer
For you say, "Peace, be still." (Mark 4:39)

Thy wondrous Holy Word makes clear
That precious in thy sight
Is the death of every saint. (Psalm 116:15)
So, won't you make it right?

This saint is young in you, I know.
Perhaps as of today.
But you have offered life to all (John 14:6)
Who, Lord, accept thy way.

The "saint" may start at eight years old,
Or may be eighty-plus.
Like vineyard workers, God grants each
The same denarius. (Matthew 20:1-16)

That does not mean that we should wait,
For death can oft come swift.

And life can be more joyful
When we accept his gift.

But, Dad, your life's behind you.
You did the best you knew.
And I have happy memories
Of days gone by with you.

Right now, our Lord stands at the door
Of Heaven, open wide.
Stop struggling, just relax in him,
And step right on inside.

A glorious, pain-free life awaits.
It's for eternity.
And, Dad, I thrill to know that you
Will many loved ones see.

Mom, too, said yes to Jesus
Very late in life.
I feel so sad that she delayed
And lived amid such strife.

But she is there to welcome you.
And guess who else you'll see?
Your mother—and your earthly dad,
Who died when you were three.

I cannot venture, Dad, to say
Who else will be "on board,"
For I don't know which friends and kin
Accepted Christ, our Lord.

But one thing that I'm certain of,
A promise for you, dear.
God swallows death forever
And wipes away each tear. (Isaiah 25:8)

He also says he's gone before
To prepare a place for you. (John 14:3)
And he will take you to himself
That you will be there, too.

So, Lord, I re-address you.
Please do not delay.
Most merciful, kind Savior,
Take my dad TODAY!

(Dad died at 5:30 that Monday afternoon, lucid to the very end. Thank you, Lord!)

❧ *TODAY'S DELIGHT:*
Write a poem to a loved one today. Tell that person how much you love him or her, and share your faith. (It doesn't need to rhyme, or be any special form, as long as it comes from the heart.) Then mail it or give it personally.

The Oil Painting

As I sit in my "prayer" chair, I glance up at a picture on the wall. When was the last time I gave any thought to that oil painting? Forty years ago, it graced the wall of my tiny living room. For a while, it hung in the rec room of our present home. It now occupies an inconspicuous spot above two file cabinets in the office.

I remember the day the picture arrived in the mail, shortly after our wedding. We didn't know the artist, but he and his wife had listened to our wedding on the "Bride and Groom" radio program. He liked what he heard and decided to paint a picture as a wedding gift for this unknown couple.

It is a simple scene—a house, trees, clouds, a blossoming tree along the banks of a swiftly flowing river.

I have no idea how Mr. Bolen of Charlotte, North Carolina, got our address. He may have sent the picture to us in care of the Hollywood program.

We never met the Bolens; however, we struck up a correspondence. Throughout the years, letters flew back and forth between North Carolina and first Idaho, then Indiana, and finally Washington. The Bolens passed along tidbits of advice, gleaned from their many years of marriage.

As I look at the picture, I realize I am nearing the age of the Bolens when they sent the lovely gift.

The Oil Painting

Then I silently ask: Is there a newly married couple
with whom I can share part of myself? It may not be a
picture to decorate a wall, but I can share words of
encouragement and love, thoughts to help them
through those early years of adjustment and struggle.

I look forward to meeting those two everyday
saints, Mr. and Mrs. Bolen, in heaven someday.

≈ *TODAY'S DELIGHT:*
Invite a newly married couple to dinner or to church
with you. Or both.

An Everyday Saint in Politics

Politics have changed the past few years. Those serving in Congress are supposed to represent their constituents. To truly represent means to "act as a spokesperson for, to serve as an example."

Several years ago, one of our state senators repeatedly challenged his coworkers by asking them, "Whom are we going to help today?"

Our family became the recipient of that help. Our daughter had accepted a government position to teach in Germany. Her possessions consisted of three shipments. She took the first batch with her. Because she packed in 100-degree weather that August, this luggage was mostly summer clothing.

Then there was the "hold" baggage. She was advised to pack one plate, one knife, one fork, one spoon, etc., to be delivered shortly after her arrival. The rest of her belongings were to reach her within two months.

Germany's weather turned chilly by mid-September, and Laurie borrowed heavier clothing. She moved into an apartment the first of October without furniture, dishes, or cooking utensils. Finally her "hold" baggage arrived. Then the wait began.

November passed—December arrived. She continued to check at the transportation office, but the answer was always, "We're investigating." Christmas came and went. Laurie concluded she'd never see her things again. Gone apparently were her furnishings for three rooms, stereo, ski equipment, to say nothing of several irreplaceable personal items.

Finally one of two crates arrived. It was marked "2000 pounds," yet it contained only her bicycle, spare tires for the car, one chair, and one stereo speaker. Had the crate been rifled through? Where was the second crate?

January—then February. Six months after Laurie's arrival in Germany, we decided to seek help on this end. I wrote to the Department of Defense and to our legislators in Washington, D.C.

The only response came from the senator mentioned above. He asked, "What can we do to help?"

In less than a week, we got a telegram from Germany and a second call from the senator's office. The missing crate was located in a Bremerhaven warehouse where it had been sitting for months. What's more—nothing was missing!

In our eyes, that senator was an everyday saint who truly cared about the "little person."

My sphere of influence is minuscule compared to someone in government. However, I need to ask myself often, "Whom am I going to help today?"

✍ *TODAY'S DELIGHT:*
Do you know a Christian serving in a governmental position? Write a note of encouragement, thanking that person for representing you, and assuring him or her of your prayers. Then be sure to pray!

"The Christian ideal," it is said, "has not been tried and found wanting; it has been found difficult and left untried."

—G. K. Chesterton
(1874–1936),
"What's Wrong
with the World?"

Delight in Values

Ideals are like stars;
you will not succeed in touching them
with your hands.
But like the seafaring man on the
desert of waters,
you choose them as your guides,
and following them you will reach your
destiny.

—Carl Schurz (1829–1906),
Address, Faneuil Hall, Boston, April 18, 1859

Zealous for God
(Enthusiasm)

It is fine to be zealous, provided the purpose is good.

(Galatians 4:18 NIV)

My uncle was deeply involved in the labor movement.
It was his life for over sixty years.
His zeal for labor took him to many parts of the world.
He was active politically, economically, and socially.
For his eightieth birthday, his children gave him a
    gold watch.
Its inscription read: *Agitate—Educate—Organize.*
Hallmarks of true zeal.

These were hallmarks of the early Christians as well.
As they got excited about Christ, they
    agitated—according to the definition, "to stir up
    public interest in a cause."
They wanted to *educate* others about
    Christ—according to the definition, "to provide with
    information, to enlighten."
And they became *organized*—according to the
    definition, "to join or form an activist group."

But make no mistake, zeal can be misdirected.
Paul wrote to the Roman Christians about the
    Israelites:
"For I can testify about them that they are zealous for

God, but their zeal is not based on knowledge"
(Romans 10:2 NIV).
Misdirected zeal!
After his arrest in Jerusalem, Paul addressed the Jews:
"I am a Jew, born in Tarsus of Cilicia, but brought up
in this city. . . .
"I was thoroughly trained in the law of our fathers and
was just as zealous for God as any of you are today"
(Acts 22:3 NIV).
Misdirected zeal!

An Indian listened to two white men discussing zeal.
One felt folks were too wishy-washy about their faith.
The other stated that zealous believers turned others
off.
They asked the Indian's opinion. He answered,
"I don't know about having too much zeal; but I think
it is better the pot should boil over than not boil at
all."
Do I have that kind of zeal . . .
zeal for my Lord,
zeal for his Word,
zeal for his cause?
I pray that my "pot" will boil over a little, rather than
not boil at all!

PRAYER:
Oh, Lord, I don't want my zeal to be misdirected. May

I "never be lacking in zeal, but keep [my] spiritual fervor, serving the Lord" (Romans 12:11 NIV).

❧ *TODAY'S DELIGHT:*
Follow the admonition in the song, "Get all excited, go tell everybody that Jesus Christ is King."[1] Do it today!

[1] Words and music by William J. Gaither. Copyright © 1972 by William J. Gaither. All rights reserved. Used by permission.

Savannah Revisited
(Gratitude)

Offer hospitality to one another.   (1 Peter 4:9 NIV)

During World War II, my husband, Kyle, was stationed at Chatham Field near Savannah and attended services at the Wesley Monumental Methodist Church. So when we visited that historic city, he was eager to see the church again. He especially had fond memories of a couple who extended dinner invitations to servicemen each Sunday.

As we approached the corner of Abercorn and Gordon Streets, Kyle exclaimed, "Why, it hasn't changed a bit!" adding wistfully, "but I'm sure the Dimmicks are no longer around."

We rang the buzzer at a side door and were met by the secretary, who graciously invited us to tour the facilities. Kyle asked about the Dimmick family.

"The parents have been dead for some years, but their son is an active member. Would you like his phone number?"

Robert Dimmick was flabbergasted—and delighted—to receive a message of appreciation for the hospitality his parents had extended to lonely servicemen over forty years ago.

Is there someone from your past—a former schoolteacher, classmate, or employer you've never thanked for a kind deed or favor? If the person is no longer alive, you can still express your gratitude to a son, daughter, or another family member.

It's never too late to say thank you.

PRAYER:
Father, help me to locate those who have befriended me in the past. I want to tell them how much I appreciated their kindness.

❧ *TODAY'S DELIGHT:*
Do exactly what you have just prayed.

"Play the Game" Honestly
(Honesty)

The LORD *detests lying lips, but he delights in men who are truthful.*   (Proverbs 12:22 NIV)

Each February, I serve as a judge for a local spelling bee. As I observe these nervous fifth through eighth graders, I remember my own elementary school days.

Winners of each grade contest advanced, first to an all-school event, then to the district, and finally to the state spelling bee. The state champion represented Michigan at the National Spelling Bee in Washington, D.C.

I won all four grade bees and in 1939 emerged a school champion. Mother drilled me nightly from word lists provided to the contestants. It paid off—I won the district!

Then came the unforgettable experience in the huge Coliseum in Detroit with fifty-four spellers from all over the state. Three judges moved from one speller to another. Soon over half the contestants were disqualified. Confidence surged through me.

"Incandescent," one judge announced.

I started slowly. "I-N-C-A-N-D-E-S-C—" *There's a tricky* C *in that word,* I thought. My voice trailed off as I added, "C-A-N-T."

The moment I finished, I knew the *A* was wrong. So

why were the judges conferring? (In those days there were no elaborate sound systems and tape recorders.) They asked me to respell the word.

"I-N-C-A-N-D-E-S-C—" I stopped suddenly.

"I spelled it wrong," I blurted out and dashed off the stage, tears blinding my eyes. Then it dawned on me. The judges hadn't heard the letter *A.* I could have given the right spelling and stayed in the contest!

I relived that horrible moment for a few days. Then I received a congratulatory note from my grandfather. In it he quoted Grantland Rice, a famous sportscaster of that day:

> *When the One Great Scorer comes*
> *to write against your name—*
> *He marks—not if you won or lost*
> *—but how you played the game.*[1]
>
> *I knew I'd done the right thing.*

PRAYER:
Lord, when I'm tempted to cheat—whether on my taxes or at a checkout counter, remind me to "play the game" honestly.

❧ *TODAY'S DELIGHT:*
Tell a child or children of a time when you enjoyed the results of practicing honesty, or the consequences of a

[1] John Bartlett, *Familiar Quotations* (Boston, Toronto: Little, Brown and Company, 1968), 961.

dishonest act. Encourage them to share with you their experiences with temptations as well as victories.

Lost Boys (Integrity)

Some months ago, two local teenage boys were reported missing. Neither returned home after working one Sunday afternoon at the gun club. Hundreds of people volunteered to help find them. Pilots conducted an air search; the sheriff's office investigated in an efficient and timely manner; the local paper and radio stations publicized the story in the hopes of gaining information about the case.

As it turned out, the boys, on a lark, decided to drive to a large city about 150 miles away, where they were spotted by the state patrol. One can only imagine the mixed emotions of both families.

Later that week, the parents of both boys published a note of appreciation in the local paper.

Underneath were two other items:

> I wish to publicly apologize to my parents, to
> _____'s parents, to the sheriff's office, to the pilots
> and spotters of the airplanes, and to the many
> friends and others who searched for me. I also
> wish to apologize to those who worried about me.
> I did not act in a responsible way, and I wish to
> learn from my mistake. Thank you for caring,
> and I ask your forgiveness.

The other item read:

> Thank you for all the time, effort, caring, and

concern that all you people used up. I realize my actions inconvenienced many people. I had no idea so many cared about two average teenagers. I apologize, and I humbly ask that you all except [sic] my apology. I promise that in the future my time will be spent more constructively. To all the kids out there who think of doing something like this, forget it. It obviously didn't get me any-where and did nothing but hurt others and humiliate me. Again all who tried to help my parents and who just worried or prayed, well, we're back and I'm sorry.

What a tribute to four parents who undoubtedly encouraged, perhaps even insisted, the boys make a public apology.

What an example of one of society's greatest missing ingredients—INTEGRITY!

❧ *TODAY'S DELIGHT:*
The next time you read an item in a magazine or newspaper about someone demonstrating integrity, send a note of appreciation. You can send it in care of the publication, and they will forward it to the proper person. Believe me, it will be appreciated.

Grand Central Station (Kindness)

And be ye kind one to another.   (Ephesians 4:32)

I stood by the phone booth in Grand Central Station. My cousin had just given me directions to Bedford Hills via commuter train.

Years before on a visit to New York City, redcaps swarmed all over this cavernous building. But now I could find no help with my heavy luggage.

A young man with glazed eyes approached me, mumbling about money. I was frightened!

God, I need help! The unspoken request formed in my mind.

I started to walk the long corridor toward Track #40, nudging one suitcase with my foot and stopping every few steps to change arms with the other bag. Glancing back, I noticed the young man following a few feet behind. I didn't like this big city!

"May I help you?" A short, roly-poly man appeared at my side.

I hesitated.

He added, "I know it's hard to trust anybody, but you really need assistance." He motioned a "go away" signal behind him, then lifted the largest suitcase and took the other from my aching arm.

"You're an answer to prayer!" I blurted out.

My benefactor smiled. Yes, he, too, believed in answered prayer. We struck a rapport that kept us chatting as he waited until my train arrived.

Kindness speaks a language that transcends geography, age, and religion. It was demonstrated to me that day in Grand Central Station as a Jewish teacher from New York City helped a Christian writer from Washington State.

We both serve a great God!

PRAYER:
Lord, give me a holy nudge when I fail to show kindness to someone needing help.

❧ *TODAY'S DELIGHT:*
Help someone with a load. It may be a clothes basket to the laundry room, an armful of books to the library, groceries from the car to the house, or dirty dishes from the table.

Intertwined Lives
(Neighborliness)

Beulah was crippled with arthritis.
Sam had always done a good job caring for her.
But now his own health was failing—and he was
  worried.
"What if I can't help her out of bed? Or down the
  stairs?"
"Call us any time of the day or night," we told him.
Our neighbor balked at the suggestion. Telephones
  intimidated him.
That's when we came up with the idea.
We devised a buzzer system between our two houses.
We strung a wire from our kitchen to the
  garage—from the garage to our neighbor's kitchen.
Sam only needed to push the buzzer. We would hear it
  and respond.
Our lives were intertwined with those of our dear
  neighbors.

Jesus gave us a far broader definition when he
  answered the lawyer's question, "Who is my
  neighbor?" (Luke 10:29 NRSV).
  The homeless on our city streets . . .
  Men and women in our prisons . . .
  AIDS victims in our hospitals . . .
  Starving Ethiopians—flood victims of

Bangladesh—orphans of Calcutta—the oppressed
in Central America . . .
All are our neighbors.

🐦 *TODAY'S DELIGHT:*
Give a tangible gift of love to your neighbor—whether
next door, across town, or across the world.

A Baker's Dozen Complex (Persistence)

Ever heard of the baker's dozen complex?
It's a characteristic of the person who says,
"I'll give it one more try."
I don't like to experience failure.
I often do, simply because I didn't try—one more time.
As Thomas Edison worked on the incandescent lamp,
   someone asked, "Why don't you give up?
"You've performed thirty thousand experiments with
   no success.
"You don't know anything more now than when you
   began."
"Oh, yes, I do," answered the famous inventor.
"I now know thirty thousand things that will *not* work."
As a writer, I'm always fascinated by stories about
   famous authors who displayed the baker's dozen
   complex.
Gustave Flaubert rewrote *Madame Bovary* at least
   three times.
He was so dissatisfied, he thought of burning the
   manuscript.
But he decided to try—one more time.
A maid *did* accidentally burn Thomas Carlyle's
   manuscript *The French Revolution*.
One day the despondent writer saw bricklayers at
   work.

A Baker's Dozen Complex

"It came to me, that as they lay brick on brick, so
    could I lay word on word, sentence on sentence."
Due to Carlyle's baker's dozen complex, he rewrote
    this monumental work.
I faced many discouraging moments writing this book.
Then I'd remember the baker's dozen complex.
I decided to go the extra mile and to try—*one* more
    time.
And after that—*one* more time again.
The result? You're holding it!

TODAY'S DELIGHT:
Are you discouraged about a project you're working on?
A relationship that's gone sour? The diet you can't stick
to? Or the lack of time you're spending in Bible study?
Tackle that problem one more time—and after that, one
more time! You'll be delighted with the results!

114

Where Are You, Myron Grundstein? (Repentance)

A California friend recently wrote me the following:

> Lord, what am I going to do about Myron Grundstein? I lied about him and I'm deeply sorry. I wish, Lord, someone had tapped my conscience long ago and called me on it! I am a senior citizen now, yet I still anguish over the incident.
>
> Myron and I were first graders and sat in the same row of attached desks. One morning, as we all sat quietly working on math problems, I started kicking the back legs of Myron's desk seat.
>
> Suddenly, I saw Miss Markley heading down the aisle, her stern face colored with anger. She stopped by Myron, bent down and demanded, "Were you kicking your desk?"
>
> Myron stiffened and his shoulders hunched toward his workbook. He shook his head, shocked that the teacher believed he was the culprit.
>
> The teacher continued, "Yes, you *were* making all that noise!" Then she looked at me. She knew she could count on me—I was reliable, courteous, helpful, and smart—my word could be trusted.
>
> "Marjorie, Myron was kicking, wasn't he?" I

could not risk Miss Markley's ill favor, so I simply nodded yes.

So Myron was held accountable for my crime. I don't know what punishment he received— whether just the scolding, no recess, or a note sent home. I only know that for sixty-plus years, I've lived with the guilt of deeply wounding an innocent six-year-old boy.

Yes, I believe that Jesus Christ has forgiven me. But my heart still cries out to the one I offended that long-ago day in a first-grade classroom in Ohio.

Myron Grundstein, please forgive me!

Marjorie has truly repented of that first grade sin, and if Myron might, perchance, read this and accept her apology, the process is complete. Regardless, Marjorie is forgiven in the sight of her Savior. And that's what counts.

❧ *TODAY'S DELIGHT:*
Search your memory. Is there someone you sinned against as a child, a teenager, a young adult, or even more recently? Go to that person and ask forgiveness. If, as in Marjorie's case, that is not possible, God will forgive any misdoings of the past. Just ask him, and you will experience the delight of his mercy.

Make It Right—
No Matter How Long It Takes!
(Restitution–1)

Yesterday I bought chicken at my favorite deli, along with several other grocery items. When I checked my sales slip, I realized the clerk had charged a mere $2.49 instead of $5.49. Some years ago, I'd have been delighted in "saving" $3.00. When I returned to the store, sales slip in hand, the manager was amazed.

The episode prompted me to check my files to see if I still had copies of two letters written in 1975. Sure enough. I'd written them anonymously, afraid to attach my name to either.

One was sent to a state university:

> Many years ago, I worked in the Radio Department of Indiana University. One of my jobs was to sort out and catalog the 78 RPM records. Discovering that there were several copies of certain selections, I did a very wrong thing. I took advantage of this duplication and took records home.

The other letter began:

> Many years ago during World War II, I worked in the chemistry lab at Great Lakes Steel. During that time, I did a very wrong thing. I took home

small bottles of carbon tetrachloride to clean my typewriter keys.

In the next paragraph of both letters, I stated:

Within the past few years, I have become a Christian and realize that, in God's eyes, this was stealing. I still didn't do anything to make amends, telling myself it happened so long ago, nobody would know the difference. But no matter how I rationalize, I must face the fact that God knows—and being right with him is the only thing that matters.

To both places, I sent a small payment. My letters continued:

There is no way of knowing the value thirty years later, but money enclosed seems to be commensurate with the amount involved. Use it for whatever need is greatest in your department at the present time.

Another eighteen years has passed, so why do I tell about these episodes? I need to publicly acknowledge these thefts, as did my dear friend Bettye in an "as told to" article I wrote for her. It has been published in several Christian publications, and Bettye gave permission to use it once again. (See the next article.)

❧ *TODAY'S DELIGHT:*
If you have "helped yourself" to office supplies at a place of employment, if you were given too much change for a purchase and kept it, if you have cheated in any way, ask God to show you how to make restitution as soon as possible.

My Persistent Lord
(Restitution–2)

by Bettye Fisher
as told to Shirley Pope Waite

I can see the scene as though it happened yesterday. The place: Murphy High School, Mobile, Alabama. The time: 1946. I even remember the blue-green dress with black stripes I wore that day.

At lunchtime, I headed for the cafeteria. If you didn't have proper change for lunch, you went to a special table. For some reason, which escapes me now, my folks had given me twenty dollars, a large sum in those days.

The student cashier counted out the change as I stood in the cafeteria line. That's when I discovered I still had the twenty-dollar bill. I looked back. Apparently the girl hadn't noticed, nor did any of my fellow students. At that point, I made a choice. I kept the money.

Occasionally through the years the incident appeared on the screen of my mind. I'd be slightly disturbed but managed to brush aside the image.

About two years ago, a friend and I were discussing a third party who became involved in theft. You can't imagine my judgmental and critical comments. Then it hit me! In God's sight, I was a thief too! In 1978, I'd accepted Christ in a personal way. Now I struggled with guilt that I'd managed to ignore for over thirty-five years!

"I want you to write to the school," God seemed to say.

"But, Lord, I haven't had any contact with Murphy High since I graduated."

"Write to the school."

"I'll drop an extra twenty dollars into the church collection plate."

"Send the school forty dollars!" came the distinct impression.

I argued with God for days.

"All right, I'll do it. But I'll mail it in Oregon." (I live six miles from the Oregon border.)

"Mail it here."

In my prayer time one morning, I gave in. "I'll mail it locally, Lord, but is it OK if I just sign my married name?"

"No, that won't do." God exposed my ridiculous games and made it crystal clear I couldn't hide from him. If I would know his forgiveness, I must not only make ample restitution, but do it his way.

On December 16, 1982, I wrote to the principal:

Dear Sir:
This may seem like a strange letter, but out of obedience to my Lord, it is one I must write. I graduated from Murphy High School in 1947.

I explained the former cafeteria practice and the circumstances of that long-ago day. Then I continued:

Four years ago I committed all of my life to the Lord. He brought this episode to mind, asking that I repay not twenty dollars, but forty dollars. I've prayed about it and know I'm to send this amount. Thank you and please use this money as you are directed.

Sincerely,
Mrs. Murray W. Fisher

With a trembling hand, I wrote underneath:

Bettye Zell Hall

After the first of the year, a receipt arrived which read, "For an old debt." There was also a note:

Hi! What a beautiful way to start a New Year! You have lots to share. Continue to do so. Love in Christ.

It was signed by the bookkeeper of Murphy High School, Mobile, Alabama.

What an affirmation from another believer hundreds of miles away! What a lesson I learned! Obedience to God brings rewards. For me, it brought freedom from guilt, and God's unconditional forgiveness. Both have deepened my faith as I strive to walk daily with him.

Friend Bettye, I want to share that your witness prompted me to write the previous devotional, "Make it Right—No Matter How Long It Takes!"

Thanks, dear sister in Christ.

🕊 *TODAY'S DELIGHT:*
Be a true "sister" or "brother" in Christ to someone struggling with temptation. Offer to stand by that person as he or she seeks to make the right decisions.

This article first appeared in *Evangel,* January 13, 1985.

Play to Win—Fairly! (Sportsmanship)

It happened during a community college women's basketball game. For some reason, the opposing team had only five players. Think of it! No bench warmers to substitute, no backup players in case of foul trouble or injury. Our school's coach, Coach W., fielded his freshmen as often as possible, which, of course, gave them added experience. However, the five opposing players became visibly exhausted.

During the second half, one of the visiting players was taken out. She was apparently experiencing a breathing problem.

According to a well-known local official, with whom I checked later, a coach can keep five players on the floor, even when the opposing team has only four remaining players.

The game was temporarily halted as Coach W. talked to the visiting coach and then to one of the referees. Without hesitation, he signaled one of his women to take the bench, leaving four local players on the gym floor with the four opposing women.

I was impressed. It's the small things that make a basketball game enjoyable for me—a coach patting a player's shoulder, a smile, a shout of encouragement, a "fair play" decision like the one made by Coach W.

We who are spectators can do our part as well— yelling for our own team, to be sure, but refraining from booing our opponents. We adults—coaches, officials, spectators—can set an example for our young people. Sportsmanship should be evident from both sides of the court or field.

🙚 *TODAY'S DELIGHT:*
Depending on the season, attend a local sports event. If no professional team is in your area, attend a high school or college game. Little League games are exciting, too. Take a friend along with you.

Pink Slips
(Success)

It was there!
The dreaded pink slip in his box!
Dick had known—ever since the government contract
    wasn't renewed.
An enclosed letter offered him early retirement.
Now reality hit him squarely between the eyes.
With a look of defeat, he handed the dreaded slip to
    Mary.
"How do you like being married to such a successful
    man?" His voice dripped with sarcasm.
My friend has a most discerning and loving wife.
She took his hand in hers.
"Dick, what's success?"
Before he could answer, she continued, "You've raised
    a great family. You've given loads of love to those
    around you.
"Your sense of humor is contagious, and others like to
    be around you.
"You've been a living example of Christianity.
"Yes, I'm married to a very successful man!"

Lord, the world measures success in terms of
    employment, dollar power, material possessions.
We don't want to fall into that trap.
Make us aware that pink slips do not measure one's
    success.

Nor does retirement from employment mean retirement from life.

❧ *TODAY'S DELIGHT:*
Do you know of someone who has lost a job, is changing employment, or is newly retired? Call or write a note. Better yet, invite that person to lunch or dinner and offer encouragement.

An Angel of Mercy
(Thoughtfulness)

Recently I read a letter to the editor in our local
newspaper. I was so impressed I contacted the writer
and asked permission to quote from it.

Because of mechanical problems, the writer and
her family ran out of gas on a lonely strip of highway
late at night. Although a few motorists stopped to say
they'd notify the highway patrol, the travelers were
helpless.

The letter stated:

> Some time after midnight, a young man going the
> opposite direction stopped his pickup and turned
> around to find out what was wrong. He said he
> would drive to the nearest town to get gas.
>
> We knew he would find nothing open at that
> time of night. What we didn't know was how
> dedicated he was to his mission of helping a
> family of strangers in the middle of the night. He
> located the chief of police, explained the
> situation, used the chief's card to get five gallons
> of gas from a city pump, and drove the twenty
> miles back to where we were stranded.
>
> As he filled our tank, he told us he had left
> your town at four o'clock in the morning to drive
> to Spokane for a golf tournament. (A distance of
> 160 miles.) Now he was on his way home, having

been up for twenty hours. When he returned
with the gas, that was stretched to twenty-one
hours, and he still had an hour's drive to get
home. He must have been exhausted.

Our five children, ages five to fourteen, were
with us. He told us he had a four-year-old
daughter and that his wife ran a day care.

We were on our way by 1:30 A.M. We don't
know his name. We pray that, tired as he was, he
got safely home. And we thank God for sending
us an angel of mercy when we needed one.

This young man was wonderful. I hope from
our description some of your readers will
recognize him and give him a pat on the back.

—Carla Gomez

A young man thoughtful enough to help a family in
need.

A young woman thoughtful enough to take the time
to publicly thank her family's "rescuer."

We need more people like this in the world, don't
you agree?

❧ *TODAY'S DELIGHT:*
Give a "warm fuzzy" to someone who has done you a
favor. It may even be a letter to the editor of your local
paper.

Delight in Holidays

The holiest of all holidays are those kept by ourselves in silence and apart;
The secret anniversaries of the heart.

— Henry Wadsworth Longfellow (1807–1882), "Holidays"

If all the year were playing holidays,
To sport would be as tedious as to work.

— William Shakespeare (1554–1616), *Henry IV,* Part I

Holidays should be like this,
Free from overemphasis,
Time for soul to stretch and spit
Before the world comes back on it.

— *Louis MacNeice*
(1907–1963), *Epilogue, for W. H. Auden*

That Beloved Saint—Patrick
(Saint Patrick's Day)

For you have been granted the privilege not only of believing in Christ but also of suffering for him.

(Philippians 1:29 NEB)

Did you know that Saint Patrick was not an Irishman by birth? He was thought to have been born in Scotland. At sixteen, he was kidnapped by Irish marauders and became a slave to a Druid chieftain. Six years later he escaped to Europe, where he became a priest. Later he felt God calling him back to Ireland to convert the pagans.

I recently heard a moving legend about this venerable saint. During baptisms, he would plunge his staff into the ground to mark the spot where newly converted people were to stand. During one service, he noticed blood running into the river.

Looking around, he saw that he had actually thrust his staff through the foot of a convert. Horrified, he asked the man, "Why didn't you cry out?"

The man answered, "I thought it was part of the baptism that I should suffer as Jesus did."

PRAYER:
Lord, most of us have never suffered for your sake. Make us willing to do so, if your name will be glorified.

That Beloved Saint—Patrick

🍀 *TODAY'S DELIGHT:*
Wear something green, perhaps a shamrock. You don't have to be Irish to celebrate the day. (If there are children in your life, make sure you wear green, or you'll get pinched!)

The Easter Cantata

*The Lord is not slow in keeping his promise. . . .
He is patient with you, not wanting anyone to
perish, but everyone to come to repentance.*

(2 Peter 3:9 NIV)

Our son was eager to have us watch a video of the
Easter cantata performed by his church. Unfortunate-
ly, the taping was done by someone who knew little or
nothing about lighting; consequently, the quality of
the video was very poor.

As family members gathered around the TV, Mark
gave a running commentary of the performance.

At one point, our granddaughter, Jessica, ran to the
screen and pointed to herself. "This is where the
children sing for Jesus."

The young man who portrayed the Christ was a
former biker with long hair who looked for all the
world like the mental image most of us have of Jesus.
The video was powerful, despite the poor quality.

The lighting in the living room didn't help either,
and the shadows of those watching were superim-
posed on the screen. I sat on the floor at my husband's feet. From my vantage point, I was suddenly
struck by a scene that will be forever etched in my
mind.

Jesus had been crucified (cleverly done with his
back to the audience), and the cantata reached its

climax. There stood the triumphant Lord, with outstretched hands as if to receive the whole world. The silhouettes of family members scattered around the room were reflected back in such a way that Jesus seemed to be embracing us all—both the saved and the unsaved!

Tears filled my eyes as the cantata drew to a conclusion and the scene disappeared before my eyes. Yet it was a message from God himself—one I so desperately needed for reassurance.

PRAYER:
Lord, give me patience as I await your perfect timing in the lives of my loved ones.

❧ TODAY'S DELIGHT:
Rent a video on the life of Christ, some other biblical character, or one depicting the Christian life-style. Invite an unsaved family member or neighbor to watch it with you. Add some popcorn and soft drinks and make it a festive occasion.

The Day of Fools
(April Fools' Day)

Ever wonder how April Fools' Day got its start? Some say its roots lie in Greek mythology. Others claim it comes from France, following the Gregorian calendar change of 1582 when the New Year was moved from March 25 to January 1. A week-long celebration ended on April 1. Frenchmen who forgot to exchange gifts or visits were ridiculed with pranks. The custom then began in the British Isles and Scotland. In Scotland, the victim of an April Fools' joke is called an "April gowk," and in France, an "April fish."

Perhaps its roots lie in the way nature fools people with capricious changes at this time of year. In a childhood book of verse, I found this poem by Eleanor Hammond (1866–1933):

> *Small April sobbed,*
> *"I'm going to cry.*
> *Please give me a cloud*
> *To wipe my eye."*
>
> *Then "April Fool!"*
> *She laughed instead,*
> *And smiled a rainbow*
> *Overhead.*

Each family has a favorite April fool joke. Perhaps when you were a child, Mother put salt in the sugar bowl, or you called out in a shocking voice to Dad, "You've got a big hole in your pants!"

My favorite trick? I inserted a piece of paper with "April Fool" written on it in the children's lunch sandwiches.

One year my son's "chowhound" friend began scrounging for more food during the lunch hour. Steve offered him a sandwich. The boy wolfed it down in seconds, making no comment. I've often wondered if he was too embarrassed to mention the "papery thin" contents, or just thought that Mrs. Waite made lousy sandwiches.

Watch out this April Fools' Day, especially if your spouse or friend serves sandwiches for lunch!

❧ TODAY'S DELIGHT:
Think of the funniest April fool joke of your past. Share it with a family member—or try it out on one of them. (Be certain it is nonthreatening and won't hurt anyone's feelings.)

"Mother" Is a Verb
(Mother's Day)

Somewhere there is a woman who gave you physical life through birth. This may or may not be the person you call "Mother." As a verb, to "mother" means to "nurture, bring up, care for, protect, shelter, watch over, keep in tow."

Countries the world over recognize that "mother" is more than a noun. Many have proverbs about the woman who knows how to "mother."

> Germany: "A good mother will not hear the
>   music of the dance when her children cry."
> France: "Mother's love is ever in its spring."
> Russia: "A mother's love will draw up from the
>   depths of the sea."
> Japan: "Buy land that slopes toward the center
>   and marry a girl whose mother is good."
> West Africa: "It is no burden for a mother to care
>   for her child."
> Israel: "God could not be everywhere, so he
>   made mothers."
> Spain: "An ounce of mother is equal to a ton of
>   priest."

Many mother-related maxims come from America. Each of us recalls what Abraham Lincoln said of his mother, "All that I am or hope to be, I owe to my angel mother." The Kentucky poet William Ross Wallace wrote the familiar words, "The hand that rocks the cradle is the hand that rules the world."

PRAYER:
God, thank you for those women who have nourished and sheltered us. Bless them on their special day.

❧ TODAY'S DELIGHT:
Do something special for one who "mothered" you. It may be the woman who gave you birth, or perhaps a teacher, friend, or neighbor. Take her to dinner, or give her a small token of your appreciation.

Known But to God
(Memorial Day)

"You must visit the American cemetery," our bed and breakfast hosts told us.

We hadn't known about this cemetery three miles from Cambridge, site of one of England's most famous universities.

Upon our arrival, we were surprised to see the American and British flags at half-mast. Special Memorial Day services were scheduled to honor the war dead buried there.

Established in 1943 on land donated by the University of Cambridge, it is the only permanent World War II military cemetery in the British Isles. The rolling grounds are framed by trees on two sides and contain 3,811 headstones in seven curved grave plots.

A large proportion of the servicemen and women buried there were crew members of British-based American aircraft. Others died in the invasion of North Africa and France, at sea, or in training areas within the United Kingdom.

An impressive Wall of the Missing lies alongside a mall with a pool bordered by roses. The wall records names of 5,125 service people missing in action—lost or buried at sea. Four huge statues carved by English craftsmen represent a soldier, sailor, airman, and coastguardsman in uniform.

A mosaic in the chapel of the memorial building

stretches across the ceiling above the altar. It depicts the archangel trumpeting the Resurrection and the Last Judgment.

As we walked reverently around the beautiful grounds, we paused at the foot of a grave. It was one of twenty-four decorated with red and white carnations tied with a blue ribbon, and flanked by tiny American and British flags. The words etched in the headstone read: "Here rests in honored glory a comrade in arms known but to God."

Tears came to my eyes as we stood in an attitude of worship. Known but to God! These service people were once known intimately by parents, siblings, friends, perhaps a spouse and children. Young men and women who fought for freedom and the dignity of mankind! Yet in death—known but to God!

Relatives and friends may forsake us. We may feel all alone in a world that offers many only poverty, cruelty, and apathy. But God knows each of us intimately. He is a husband to the widow—"For thy Maker is thine husband; the LORD of hosts is his name" (Isaiah 54:5). He is a father to the orphan—"A father of the fatherless . . . is God in his holy habitation" (Psalm 68:5). He is Father to us all!

Known but to God! Isn't that the most important relationship of any? Thank God, we are known to him, not just in life, not just in death, but for eternity!

🍃 *TODAY'S DELIGHT:*
Decorate the grave of a loved one, or offer to drive a
friend to the cemetery to take flowers.

First appeared in *Decision,* May 1986

Honor Thy Father
(Father's Day)

Honor thy father . . . as the LORD thy God hath commanded thee. (Deuteronomy 5:16)

I'm rather proud that Father's Day originated in my state of Washington. Let me tell you the story.

It all started one Sunday morning back in 1909 when Mrs. John Bruce Dodd listened to a Mother's Day sermon. She found herself thinking about her father, William Smart, affectionately known as "Billy Buttons." He had raised her and her five brothers single-handedly on their eastern Washington farm after their mother died at an early age.

It isn't fair that mothers are honored but not fathers, she thought. Then, suddenly, she straightened up in her pew: *Why don't I do something about it?*

She told her pastor about her idea, and together they proposed to the Spokane Ministerial Association a new holiday, one that honored fathers. The YMCA agreed to publicize it. Thus, in 1910 Spokane was the first city in the United States to honor fathers on a special day. In 1916 President Woodrow Wilson participated in a Father's Day celebration by pressing a button in Washington, D.C. that unfurled a flag in Spokane. Then in 1924 President Coolidge recommended that the third Sunday in June be set aside to honor fathers. Thirty-three years later, Senator Margaret Chase Smith tried to have the day officially recognized. I was surprised to learn that it wasn't until 1972 that Father's Day was established permanently when President Nixon signed a Congressional resolution.

Mrs. Dodd was not opposed to giving gifts to Dad. Back in 1910, she suggested Spokane merchants display gifts. "The gift idea was included in the original program and is as old as the day itself," she said. "I'm convinced that it's a sacred part of the holiday as the giver is spiritually enriched in the tribute paid his or her father."

Someone asked Mrs. Dodd how Father's Day should be spent. She answered, "It should include family attendance at church, a little gift for Dad, and some tender words you've always longed to say to him."

Today I'm going to concentrate on remembering the many unspoken ways my dad loved me. He is no longer living, but my son is now a father. I can let him know how I appreciate the way he is raising my grandchildren.

PRAYER:
Father God, thank you for the gifts of fathers everywhere. May you bless and inspire their lives today and always.

Honor Thy Father

❧ *TODAY'S DELIGHT:*
Follow Mrs. Dodd's advice. Go to church. Give a little gift to either your own father or someone special in your life who is a father. Share what's on your heart with that person.

An Attitude of Gratitude
(Independence Day)

Remember back to 1976—when we celebrated our country's Bicentennial?

Remember the patriotic fervor that sprang up all over America? Compare that to more recent celebrations, perhaps in your own family. Did you look forward to Independence Day as a time to catch up on sleep, to garden, or to have a barbecue in your backyard? You might have gone to a ball game, a picnic at the park, or even watched fireworks in the evening. Were you thankful for these opportunities?

In 1826, at the time of our semicentennial anniversary, people were disillusioned about the way this fiftieth birthday was being celebrated. A newspaper of the day commented that the usual celebration was "by frying chicken, firing away damaged powder, or fuddling our noses over tavern wine." In Washington, D.C., a committee busily prepared special festivities. They decided to invite all living former presidents and signers of the Declaration of Independence. This included John Adams, Thomas Jefferson, James Madison, James Monroe, and Charles Carroll.

Adams, who was asked to propose a toast, couldn't attend, but sent the following words to be given in his absence. "It is my living sentiment and by the blessing of God it shall be my dying sentiment—independence now and independence forever!"

A collection was also taken to help the absent Thomas Jefferson pay off a debt he had incurred when endorsing a note for a bankrupt friend.

News traveled slowly then, and two days after this charitable gesture, word reached the capital city that Jefferson had died on July 4. Then on July 8 it was learned that Adams also died on Independence Day. Ironically, five years later, James Monroe died on July 4. Americans felt that this was Divine Providence and July 4 brought a new significance to our ancestors.

We've had over 215 years of freedom that many countries in the world have just begun to experience. Let's cultivate an attitude of gratitude, remembering that living in America, despite its problems, far surpasses what's second best!

🕊 *TODAY'S DELIGHT:*
Make a note on your calendar to fly the flag on all legal public holidays, as well as on election days.

Returning to the Workplace
(Labor Day)

And the shepherds returned, glorifying and praising God for all the things that they had heard and seen, as it was told unto them. (Luke 2:20)

Smiles broke out when the congregation noticed that Luke 2 was the Scripture reading Labor Day Sunday. What did the Christmas story have to do with Labor Day? Surely the secretary had made a typographical error.

The pastor began, "You know the familiar story—angels appearing to the shepherds, and their decision to go to Bethlehem to 'see this thing which is come to pass, which the Lord hath made known unto us.' The end of the story is often overlooked. 'And the shepherds returned.'

"These simple folk had just seen a miraculous sight—the long-awaited Messiah! What a privilege! What a joy! But the shepherds realized they couldn't stay at the manger worshiping the Christ child; they had to return to work." The pastor's Labor Day sermon followed.

Each of us has a "workplace"—the office, the factory, the classroom, the home, or somewhere in the out-of-doors. For the retired, it may be a volunteer job. After a holiday or a "spiritual high" such as the shepherds experienced, those jobs may be the *last* thing we want to do. But like the shepherds, let's return to our workplaces "glorifying and praising God."

PRAYER:
Lord God, whatever my work, may I do it with joy and renewed hope for the future.

🔊 *TODAY'S DELIGHT:*
Set aside some time to pray for your "workplace." You might pray for a coworker, for the grace to do an unpleasant task without grumbling, or God's blessings on your physical surroundings. Pray rejoicing!

The Happiest Halloween

This story was told to me by Jeanne Zepeda. It happened to her family several years ago.

The children all still remember their happiest Halloween. It was—believe it or not—the year I was stretching a support check to feed, clothe, and shelter five foster children, plus my own two little girls.

That fall I asked myself impatiently, "Why does Halloween come on the last day of the month?" I planned and budgeted so carefully, yet we existed on beans, potatoes, and corn bread the week before each check arrived.

And here it was October 31—an exciting time in the life of any child. So how could I explain to the seven they couldn't participate in this fun night? I hadn't reckoned with their ingenuity. The two oldest foster children rummaged through the apartment and, with worn pillowcases and makeup, managed to outfit the five younger boys and girls.

"But, kids, we don't have anything to give—" I was interrupted.

"Mom, just wait and see!" I stayed in the background and watched.

As the last streaks of light disappeared from the sky, thirteen-year-old Judy Ann herded the younger ones out the back door to begin the rounds of our housing project. (In those days, it was perfectly safe to allow the children to go out by themselves.) Fifteen-year-old James manned the front door, telling early arrivals, "Come back in half an hour."

Before long, I heard noises in the kitchen. The youngsters rushed in, dumped their sacks of candy and gum into a big bowl and dashed out again. James was soon offering the "trick or treaters" goodies from the bowl. He was later joined by his four siblings and my two preschoolers as the giggly "ghosts" took turns passing out treats.

When the last "beggar" had rung the doorbell, I was as surprised as the children to count three sacks of candy left over.

All seven are now grown with families of their own, yet that long-ago Halloween always brings back happy memories for them. As for me, it was a beautiful example of something I'd read in the Bible:

> For if you give, you will get! Your gift will return to you in full and overflowing measure, pressed down, shaken together to make room for more, and running over. Whatever measure you use to give—large or small—will be used to measure what is given back to you. (Luke 6:38 TLB)

🍂 *TODAY'S DELIGHT:*
Help a child carve a jack-o'-lantern.

Thanksgiving—Then and Now

And now said the Governor gazing
Abroad on the piled-up stores
Of sheaves that dotted the clearings
And covered the meadows o'er . . .

That's all I remembered of the poem. Then not long ago, I found a yellowed sheet of notebook paper with the words to *The First Thanksgiving Day*—A.D. 1621. Had I actually memorized those forty-eight lines as a grade schooler? As I reread this colonial ballad, other long forgotten words jumped out:

And therefore, I, William Bradford
By the grace of God today . . .

Maidens and dames of Plymouth,
Your delicate crafts employ . . .

For the grave of sweet Rose Standish
O'ershadowed Thanksgiving Day . . .

But the final verse took me by surprise.

Massasoit the Sachem . . .
With a blow on his chest,
Muttered, "The good great spirit
Loves his white children best."

Were the words historically correct? I checked. Sure enough, the Indian did mutter that statement.

How do you suppose the Pilgrims reacted? Did they think of their flight from religious persecution? The sixty-five days' crossing on the Mayflower? The half of their number who perished the previous winter? Or perhaps that this feast was in overwhelming thanks to the providence of that "Great Spirit"?

Then I wondered—if someone from a Third World country were to enter my home on Thanksgiving Day, might that person say, "the good Great Spirit loves his American children best"? Would I apologize for the abundance? Would I explain that our first president issued a proclamation for a national day of thanksgiving in 1789 to thank God for America's blessings? Would I say, "Join us, brothers and sisters"?

Above all, would I remember the words of Jesus, "Much is required from those to whom much is given, for their responsibility is greater" (Luke 12:48 TLB).

ᢠ *TODAY'S DELIGHT:*
Plan to help at a community Thanksgiving dinner for the underprivileged. Or give generously to a Thanksgiving basket project, through your church or a charitable organization. If none of these opportunities is available, invite someone less fortunate into your home for Thanksgiving dinner. (You might want to do both!)

The First Candle
(Advent)

It was the first Sunday in Advent.

One of the church families read the Scripture, lit the first candle, and explained its symbolism.

The minister then reminded us that many would reenact this simple but meaningful ceremony in their homes later in the day.

How my heart ached as I thought ahead to the evening. We had always followed the Advent tradition of lighting candles, singing carols, and saying a prayer with our children.

Now, for the first time, there would be only my husband and me. Would I break down as I looked at the old printed Advent service, wrinkled and worn with use, with the children's names penciled in? Was it worth the bother? No, we could forego it tonight.

Why light the angel chimes and other Christmas candles? Why go through the whole ritual for just the two of us?

About nine that evening, my husband turned from the TV set and said, "Are we going to do our thing?"

"I guess so," I responded weakly.

As we passed the printed service back and forth, a lump grew in my throat. However, as "Father" asked "Mother" to light the first candle, I felt an imperceptible quickening in my spirit, a growing sense of joy beyond the pain in my heart.

Why, I thought, the coming of Christ is not just a feeling. It's a *knowing*, no matter what age or stage I pass through.

I smiled, and lit the first candle—the candle of "hope."

🙠 *TODAY'S DELIGHT:*
If you haven't already done so, begin an Advent service in your home. Check with your church or Christian bookstore for materials.

First appeared in *Sunday Digest*, November 28, 1982.

Christopher Robin Claus
(Christmas)

*Look! I have been standing at the door, and I am
constantly knocking. If anyone hears me calling
him and opens the door, I will come in and
fellowship with him and he with me.*

(Revelation 3:20 TLB)

Our great-granddaughter is a Winnie-the-Pooh fan.
When asked who was coming on Christmas Eve, she
adamantly answered, "Christopher Robin!" Not even a
trip to visit a department store Santa Claus could
dissuade her.

Then Santa actually visited her home (in the guise
of our son-in-law, her grandfather). From that point,
we heard no more of Christopher Robin. Now Santa
took center stage as the bona fide "toy bringer."

It reminds me of those years I went to church
faithfully and led a good, "moral" life. I heard Jesus'
name mentioned from the pulpit and even read his life
story in the Bible. Then I met him personally, and he
became my "blessing bringer" as well as my "burden
bearer," "problem solver," and "decision maker."

He is now center stage in my life. That's why the
Christmas season has become more meaningful to me
than ever.

Is Jesus still standing at the door of your life? This

holy season is an ideal time to invite him in from the wings and let him take center stage.

PRAYER:
Lord, as we anticipate the celebration of your birth, meet us at the point of our every need and fill us with joy each day.

🕊 *TODAY'S DELIGHT:*
Read Clement Moore's classic 'Twas the Night before Christmas *to your favorite child. Then thoughtfully read Peter Marshall's* Let's Keep Christmas *as a reading gift to yourself.*

Delight in Friendship

Oh, the comfort, the inexpressible comfort of feeling safe with a person; having neither to weigh thoughts nor measure words, but to pour them all out, just as they are, chaff and grain together, knowing that a faithful hand will take and sift them, keep what is worth keeping, and then, with the breath of kindness, blow the rest away.

—George Eliot
(1819–1880)

So long as we love, we serve; so long as we are loved by others, I should say that we are almost indispensable; and no man is useless while he has a friend.

*—R. L. Stevenson
(1850–1894)*

Closer Than Kin

Some friends play at friendship but a true friend sticks closer than one's nearest kin.

(Proverbs 18:24 NRSV)

She was more than a friend. She was a fellow writer, an encourager, a confidante, a dynamic Christian, a true sister in Christ. All of these, and more.

I first met Lois Henderson when we were roommates at a special workshop sponsored by a well-known magazine. We became soul mates and established a "tapespondence," as Lois called it. It was an ideal way to stay in touch since she was blind in one eye.

Lois had just become established as a biblical fiction writer with her first novel, *Hagar.* Through the ensuing years, she tried out her ideas on me, and I always thrilled to read the finished product. *Ruth, Miriam, Abigail,* and *Lydia* followed in swift succession, causing one editor to comment that Lois was probably the most gifted and craftsmanlike writer of biblical fiction on the contemporary scene.

Craftsmanship was her byword! She told writing students, "You are not just an inspired artist. You are a technician and must learn to be meticulous."

Many people were under the impression that Lois hit it lucky at fifty-nine when *Hagar* was published. That always amused her. She told me, "You can begin a new career at sixty as long as you're willing to practice for thirty years before." Yet, she was equally adamant about encouraging people of any age to make a start.

I was one of those people she encouraged. She was painfully honest and once told me, "When I started, I had everything backwards. It never occurred to me to ask God's guidance first. I'd write and then pray, 'Please, God, let me find an editor who will buy my stuff.' When I began to write biblical novels, I discovered my priorities were reversed. I simply couldn't write fiction based on the Bible without the indwelling presence of the Holy Spirit. And my personal life has changed. I'm more aware of God's guidance and how he wants me to share with others what he's taught me."

She was eager for just such an opportunity when asked, in 1983, to be a featured writer at the Christian Booksellers' Association convention. Dashing into the Pittsburgh airport that July 16 for her flight to Washington, D.C., her heart suddenly stopped. What she'd called an opportunity of a lifetime became, instead, an opportunity to spend eternal life with her Lord.

PRAYER:
May I, Father, like my friend Lois, always seek your guidance in order to share with others what you have taught me.

🐦 *TODAY'S DELIGHT:*
What are your special skills? Carpentry? Cooking?
Entertaining? Visiting nursing homes? Share a bit of
advice with another seeking to serve God in the area of
your expertise.

A Labor of Love

Bear one another's burdens, and so fulfil the law of Christ.

(Galatians 6:2 RSV)

It happened years ago after I'd had major surgery. Church members brought food for my family, not only when I was in the hospital, but for several days after I returned home. In addition, I received many cards and phone calls.

Then came those long days of recuperation when I could barely manage to care for my young family, much less do housework.

One frustrating afternoon as I rested on the davenport, gazing at a spiderweb on the ceiling, the doorbell rang. There stood Mary with a bucket, mop, and disinfectant.

"I've come to clean your bathroom," she announced.

You've got to be kidding! I thought. I began to protest, but she was insistent.

"I've got boys at my house too, and I know bathrooms need a regular scrubdown." Frankly, I was embarrassed and continued to object. She looked me straight in the eye and said, "Please consider this my love gift to you."

An offer to clean the yukkiest room in the house! I've never received a more appreciated gift! I doubt that Mary realized her "labor of love" was a fulfillment of Christ's law to bear another's burdens.

PRAYER:
Lord, thank you for thoughtful folks like Mary. May I also be a "burden bearer."

&. *TODAY'S DELIGHT:*
Furnish a meal or perform a much-needed chore for someone who has just come home from the hospital. If nobody comes to mind, do something special for a shut-in.

Miss Loretta

As a writer, I've been asked if I ever became a pen pal with anyone who wrote to me.

Yes, as a matter of fact. I always answer letters, yet rarely continue a correspondence due to lack of time. But Loretta Lohmuller was an exception.

Over thirty years ago when my youngest son was an infant, this maiden lady from Baltimore wrote me. It was my first fan letter, in response to my first published piece. I was thrilled to know my writing had touched someone. I replied immediately and told her a little about my family.

"Miss Loretta" began to send gifts to my son. She never missed Valentine's Day, Easter, Christmas, or his birthday. Each item was uniquely geared for his age. As Steve grew older, he eagerly looked forward to the little packages, as well as her frequent notes. Both stopped arriving shortly after he started school.

A few months later, I received a letter from Loretta's widowed sister, Bess Freseman. "Miss Loretta" was now with her Lord.

But that isn't the end of the story. Bess picked up where her sister left off. There were no more gifts for a little boy—that was "Miss Loretta's" special calling. But Bess began sending me copies of a column she wrote for *The Bell,* her church newsletter. In fact, she added my name to their mailing list.

How I enjoyed her column "The Quiet Corner," in

which she shared episodes from childhood days and beautiful memories of her older sister. I came to know "Miss Loretta" more intimately long after her death.

I also felt a small part of Saints Stephen and James' Lutheran Church in Baltimore, as I read of Pastor Thompson and parish activities.

Then Bess's letters stopped. My name remained on *The Bell*'s mailing list for a while, so I later read the lovely tribute to Bess Freseman.

I never met these sisters, Loretta and Bess. I never saw a picture of them. Yet I believe we will one day recognize each other and renew the friendship that began over thirty years ago.

🍂 *TODAY'S DELIGHT:*
Write a "fan" letter. It may be to your favorite author (c/o the publishing company). Or perhaps warm words to an elected official who has taken a courageous stand, a courteous clerk, even your pastor. The possibilities are endless. You may not receive an answer, but then again, who knows what the outcome may be?

No Generation Gap

The young woman and I had known each other less than two years when she moved away. Yet strong ties of love existed between us.

She recently returned for a three-day visit. There were dozens of people for her to see, but she came to my home, and for two hours we basked in each other's presence.

We recalled the time we traveled to a writers' conference together. She'd arranged my lodging in the guest room of a women's dormitory, greatly reducing my expenses. All the way home, we giggled like children over hilarious episodes that took place during the conference and in the dorm.

I remember the year she attended our local retreat at a mountain camp. She arose early to wash her hair, and the hair dryer blew a fuse. We searched indoors for the fuse box—no luck—then outdoors around the rustic cabin, during a rainstorm. We found it after getting soaking wet. It wasn't funny at the time, but now it added to our storehouse of humorous and poignant memories.

We come from different backgrounds, religions, experiences. Our only mutual interest seems to be our love of writing. I'm even old enough to be her mother! Yet I believe God arranged this friendship. Come to think of it—our love for him is, indeed, the greatest thing we have in common.

As she left, I thought of a short poem written by the Persian poet, Anwar-I-Saheili:

Am I united with my friend in heart,
What matters if our place be wide apart?

So I thank my kind and gentle friend for allowing me to be one of the "older" women in her life.

🙠 *TODAY'S DELIGHT:*
Invite someone from a generation other than your own to lunch or another type of get-together. Work at culti-vating this friendship.

169

My Nonagenarian Friend

Cast me not off in the time of old age; forsake me not when my strength faileth. (Psalm 71:9)

My friend Midge turned ninety this week.
There will be a special birthday party at the church.
I look at Midge Sunday mornings and think . . .
Midge doesn't look that old! Is it possible that I, too, can live an active and creative life into my nineties?
Midge worked in a chiropractor's office until she was almost eighty years old.
Her soothing voice eased patients' tensions as much as the ultrasound machine she operated.
Midge still maintains a home and garden.
She says, "I spend more time with God now in my garden because I can only do it on my knees. Sometimes I need a little push to get going, but his hand is right in back doing the pushing."

Lord, I take delight in Midge's sense of humor and positive outlook.
I admire her daily affirmation that you are with her and will always answer.
Help me to rely on your strength when my own is in short supply.

🍃 *TODAY'S DELIGHT:*
Go into your yard and pull some weeds without
complaining. If it's not the gardening season, scrub a
floor. While on your knees, spend the time with God.

Since this was written, Midge has gone to be with her Lord. Her
memorial service was truly generational—the very young up
through her contemporaries, over two hundred in all.

A Friend for My Husband

We have sworn friendship with each other in the name of the LORD.   (1 Samuel 20:42 NIV)

David and Jonathan had a unique relationship with each other, an enviable friendship between two men. Perhaps I'm mistaken, but it seems to me it's easier for a woman to establish an in-depth bond with another woman than for a man to enjoy that same closeness to another man.

Throughout the years, I've always had a harmonious rapport with two or three women friends. And I coveted a similar fellowship for my husband.

Oh, he had coworkers with whom he fished, but he confessed he wasn't comfortable with their drinking and coarse language.

And then Den came along. A fellow Christian, Kyle met Den at church and discovered their mutual love of fishing. Young enough to be Kyle's son, Den was very watchful of my husband. They'd return from a fishing trip with hair-raising stories, yet I never worried about Kyle.

Den operates a business downtown, while my husband is retired. A 10:00 A.M. coffee break has become a daily ritual. Each Wednesday morning at 7:00, they meet with others for a prayer breakfast, and they belong to the same men's Sunday school Bible study.

Kyle's spiritual life has blossomed since Den came into his life. As their friendship and loyalty to each other deepens, so does their love for God.

PRAYER:
How grateful I am, Lord, for the friend you have provided for my husband. Thank you for our friends of all ages.

🍃 *TODAY'S DELIGHT:*
Whether you have one special friend or several, make an effort to cultivate a friendship with someone new to you—a neighbor, coworker, a church member.

My Best Friend

Had you asked me to name my best friend over the years, my answer might have been Donna, Kay, Dolores, or Betty.

Today I'm more likely to answer, "My husband is my best friend." Perhaps that should have been my response right from the beginning of our courtship and romance, certainly from the beginning of our married life. But I never thought of him as one to whom I could tell my inmost thoughts, share my victories, and confess my failures. For all those years, he remained on the outside looking in, so to speak.

Oh, we talked—not always in agreement—about our children, our finances, our extended families, our work outside the home.

After we finally achieved an empty nest, I thought, *What can we say to each other, except "Please pass the salt"?*

There have been changes during these retirement years. Some have been on Kyle's part (see preceding meditation), but I've changed too.

For a while, our cat, Pippin, served as a mutual point of interest. This strange black feline gave us lots to talk about. She hated strangers. When the front doorbell rang, she'd scoot down to the basement. If she heard the back doorbell, which blocked her way downstairs, she'd run to the bedroom, and as slick as a whistle, shimmy up under the bedspread, not

realizing she made a hump in the middle of the bed.
Pippin was small but mighty, not allowing a dog or any
other cat on our property. She provided an unending
source of material for conversation.

But Pippin is gone. So are my preconceived ideas
that a "best friend" should be of the same sex. Today,
my husband and I share comfortably. We still might
not agree on every subject, but that's the case with
most of my female friends.

Today, I can unequivocally state, "Kyle, my dear
husband, aside from the Lord Jesus, you are my best
friend!"

≥ *TODAY'S DELIGHT:*
*Write a love note to your spouse, acknowledging him or
her as your best friend. Place it on your spouse's pillow,
or some unusual spot, such as your husband's fishing
tackle box, or your wife's sewing basket. Or how about
with your husband's razor, or your wife's makeup? If you
are single, write a note of appreciation to someone who
serves as your confidante—your best friend.*

Sister Days

It was noon when Joyce brought me home from our monthly writers' meeting. We sat in the car talking about our families, our writing successes and failures, and world problems.

Suddenly I saw my son coming home from school. Had we actually talked that long? Joyce squeezed my hand and said, "Just consider this a 'sister day.'"

I need more "sister days." I get so involved with activities, I feel guilty when I take time to visit. Then I thought of my great-grandmother's era. She had no car or phone. Most of her waking hours were spent in day-to-day survival. Yet she and her friends had quality time in their sharing that turned quilting bees, weddings, and christenings into "sister days."

Perhaps I could visit a friend when we both have mending to do, or enjoy a "sister day" while stuffing envelopes for the church. Even if my visit is not spent performing some task, I shouldn't feel guilty. Taking time for friendship is an accomplishment in itself.

This is going to be a busy week. But I'm going to contact Nancy, who is struggling with depression. I can turn an hour with her into a "sister day."

PRAYER:
Lord, make me aware that time spent with a friend
can be as creative and meaningful as writing a poem
or painting a picture.

❧ *TODAY'S DELIGHT:*
*Plan a "sister day" in the near future. Working folks can
turn a lunch hour or an evening slice of time into a
"sister (or brother) day."*

First appeared in *Come Celebrate* (Lynnwood, Wash.: Aglow
Publications, 1984).

My Sympathy Message

I struggled to find the words to write on a sympathy card to a friend who had lost her husband. Four years earlier her only son had died in a freak accident.

Then I remembered a poem I'd once written. In fact, I'd tried to sell it to the greeting card companies with no success. I typed it up and included it in the card.

Lettice contacted me immediately to say how much my words had meant to the whole family. She asked if the poem could be used in the memorial bulletin to be handed out at the funeral.

Here it is:

God's plan is good, whate'er men say,
We see His wonders, day by day.
A child is born, a joy to see,
Each one a gift, dear Lord, from Thee.

A mate we choose from all the rest.
Our love and patience meet the test.
A sacred thing in life of man,
This, too, is part of God's great plan.

If we believe that God is love,
'Tis also true when, from above,
He calls a dear one to abide
With Him, in Heaven, by His side.

Oft'times this part of God's great plan
Is cursed and misconstrued by man.
But faith He sends from that dim shore
To say we live forevermore.

Since that time, I've included the poem in the sympathy cards I send. I thank God for giving me these words that have brought a measure of comfort to many.

TODAY'S DELIGHT:
The next time you send a sympathy card, ask God to give you a personal message for those who mourn. I would be delighted if you wish to use my poem. My only request is that you put my name and the name of this book (Shirley Pope Waite, Delight in the Day*) at the bottom for credit.*

Rake, Rojo, and Upsidario

Don't laugh! Those names belonged to my imaginary playmates of long ago. I must have been three or four when Rake, Rojo, and Upsidario first joined me at my child-sized table for tea and toast. After all, there were three other chairs, and my tea set provided plates and cups for four. To this day, I don't know the sex of my three playmates, nor could I describe anything else about them. I just know they were my constant companions until, at the age of five, my younger brother was born. Shortly thereafter, I started school and discovered playmates with skin on.

A few years ago, a study at Yale University found that up to 70 percent of children under five have imaginary friends. They concluded that children with fantasy companions tend to be brighter, show more ability to concentrate, and are generally happier.

Even though many of these children had no siblings, researchers also concluded such youngsters probably don't invent their friends out of loneliness. Rather, a child looks upon an imaginary pal as a true protector, best listener, the most loyal friend, and an obedient servant.

Today I have another unseen Friend. He is with me, not only during tea and toast, but at all times. Since I invited this Friend to be my constant companion, I've discovered he is a true protector, the one who listens to me best, a loyal friend, and an ideal example of obedient servanthood.

The child Shirley says, "Hurrah for Rake, Rojo, and Upsidario!"

The adult Shirley says, "Hurrah for Jesus Christ!"

❧ *TODAY'S DELIGHT:*
Allow a preschooler in your life to introduce you to his or her imaginary playmate. Or recall your own "pretend" friend, and thank God for the gift of imagination.

Triumphant Entry

For we know that if the earthly tent we live in is destroyed, we have a building from God, a house not made with hands, eternal in the heavens.

(2 Corinthians 5:1 NRSV)

She was my matron of honor. We'd met when we were both working at rival radio stations, but we soon became fast friends. When my husband and I were dating and rarely had money for entertainment, Doris and her husband frequently invited us into their small rented home.

We married, moved, and I almost lost track of my friend. We then learned she had divorced and moved to California, where she made a name for herself on the fringes of Hollywood. Her devotion to her dog was the theme of each Christmas letter, and my children always identified her as "the lady with the dog."

I don't know whether it was before or after she married Bob, but her yearly letter changed dramatically. Instead of her dog, Doris talked about her Lord. No pussyfooting around either, as she urged all of her friends to consider the evidence of the man called Jesus Christ.

We were delighted to meet Bob during a visit in 1989. I accompanied Doris to a Christian women's event and witnessed her enthusiasm for God's work.

The Christmas letter of 1991 arrived. She had been

diagnosed with leukemia and spent several weeks in a completely sterilized plastic-enclosed room. Yet the letter ended on a triumphant note: "We are convinced that everything is in God's hands. What a wonderful feeling!"

Remission followed, and with it, hope for the future.

Then Doris sent me a copy of their church newsletter in which she thanked her friends for cards, visits, and donated blood, as well as for friendship, love, and prayers. She told them the leukemia had returned.

"Both Bob and I trust the Lord completely, and we are ready to be conformed to his will. In the meantime, we also want to be conformed to Christ's image. I am totally at peace with God's plan, whatever it is."

I received that letter July 9.

A couple of weeks later, the following note arrived:

Dear Folks,
Doris went to be with the Lord on the ninth of July. She didn't seem to have much pain, but could not resist an infection. While I miss her so much, I know she is far better off now just praising the Lord and basking in His glory.
Fondly,
Bob

I wrote to Bob for permission to use this material. He replied, "Doris would be most pleased," and added, "Doris was witnessing to a student nurse the day before she died. She asked Cynthia if she knew Jesus, and then asked me to follow up because she (Doris) was so weak. What a great memory for me, that during this ordeal, she would proclaim her mighty Lord to a lost soul."

I am saddened by her death; yet I am keenly aware that one day my earthly tent shall also be destroyed. But when I have that new eternal house, I shall join Doris and other saints in praising our wonderful God.

PRAYER:
Lord, help me to say with the apostle Paul, "For to me, to live is Christ and to die is gain" (Philippians 1:21 NIV).

≈ *TODAY'S DELIGHT:*
Share something of your faith in your Christmas correspondence. If it's not the holiday season, you can do the same in the next letter you write.

Active Fingers

*You will come to the grave in full vigor, like
sheaves gathered in season.*   (Job 5:26 NIV)

My friend Dorothy was an invalid.
At least, that's how most people would describe her.
A heart condition kept her confined to her home.
Sitting in an easy chair, an afghan covering her legs,
   she spoke of more active days.
"My legs hardly support me anymore, my eyesight is
   rotten, but I still exercise these every day."
She spread her fingers apart.
Her husband laughed. "Dorothy has the most
   vigorous fingers of anybody I know."
I knew what he meant.
Dorothy used those fingers to call folks "less
   fortunate than I am"—widows, cancer victims,
   those suffering depression.
She was an active member of a prayer chain.
The telephone was her contact with hurting people.
Dorothy's heart stopped beating last year.
But those "vigorous fingers" remained active until her
   harvesttime.
Our age or physical condition doesn't matter, does it,
   Lord? At fifty, seventy, or ninety, we can still serve
   you.

Just keep my spirit vigorous as you did my friend
   Dorothy.
That's the part that will go on living and serving you.

࿔ *TODAY'S DELIGHT:*
*Activate your fingers and call a shut-in or someone who
needs a friend today.*

The word of God is something alive and active: it cuts like any double-edged sword but more finely: it can slip through the place where the soul is divided from the spirit, or joints from the marrow; it can judge the secret emotions and thoughts.

—Hebrews 4:12
(Jerusalem Bible)

Delight in God's Word

The Anvil

Last eve I passed beside a
   blacksmith's door,
And heard the anvil ring the vesper
   chime;
Then looking in, I saw upon the floor
Old hammers, worn with beating
   years of time.

"How many anvils have you had,"
   I said,
"To wear and batter all these
   hammers so?"
"Just one," said he, and then with
   twinkling eye,
"The anvil wears the hammers out,
   you know."

Continued

And so, thought I, the anvil of God's
  Word,
For ages skeptic blows have beat
  upon;
Yet though the noise of falling blows
  was heard,
The anvil is unharmed . . . the
  hammers gone.

—Author Unknown

Eleven Bibles

Oh, how I love your law! I meditate on it all day long.
(Psalm 119:97 NIV)

Eleven Bibles sit on my coffee table. Yes, eleven! The largest is two and a quarter inches high, and the smallest is three quarters of an inch high.

As a youngster, I played with these miniature books whenever we visited my grandparents. When Granddad was in the British navy and stationed on the Rock of Gibraltar, he whiled away the lonely hours by carving the set of Bibles from limestone. A cross is carved on each "cover" and "spine." Gilt is still visible on the indented "pages."

My mother inherited the Bibles and, knowing my penchant for them, sent me the set one Christmas. Occasionally I still handle the tiny "books" lovingly as I did when I was a child. For years I also picked up the small leather Bible Granddad gave me in much the same way—lovingly, but only occasionally.

Then through a study group, I began making Bible reading a daily habit. Now I thrill to the treasures found within the eleven translations and paraphrases of Holy Scripture—yes, eleven—on my bookshelves.

Eleven Bibles

PRAYER:
Father, thank you for the inexpressible privilege of
Bible ownership and for the joy of studying your Word.

❧ TODAY'S DELIGHT:
*If you have only one version of the Holy Scriptures,
obtain a different translation or paraphrase from your
church or public library. Choose a few favorite verses
and enjoy comparing them.*

After the Fact

We were gone for three months one summer.
Can you imagine the pile of magazines awaiting me
    upon our return?
What slow going, trying to catch up on all of them,
    and what frustration . . .
Reading articles in late November on such subjects as
Christian athletes going to the summer Olympics . . .
Issues Christians should be aware of before voting . . .
Interviews with the presidential candidates . . .
World developments in the Middle East.
Everything I read was "after the fact."
Later when I picked up my Bible, I read about
witnessing . . .
feeding the hungry and clothing the naked . . .
turning the other cheek . . .
forgiving those who have harmed me.
Too often I read these things "after the fact" . . .
after I've let the opportunity pass to share my faith . . .
after I've ignored pleas from the local Christian aid
    center . . .
after I've reacted to an unkind remark . . .
after I've harbored a grudge toward one who has hurt
    me.
I need to keep current with the news
if I am to be a knowledgeable and contributing citizen.
I also need to stay in the Word daily
if I am to be a servant of the living God.

🍂 *TODAY'S DELIGHT:*
Set aside an hour or so each week to read current
magazines coming into your home. Browse through the
Table of Contents and first choose articles that most
directly affect and/or interest you.

Covering Statement

You will be secure, because there is hope.

(Job 11:18 NIV)

As we went through customs at Narita Airport in Tokyo, I noticed airline attendants placing stickers on the luggage. One of the bright yellow stickers was also placed on my carry-on bag.

When we were well on our way aboard the huge 747 plane, I took my Bible out and settled down to read. About that time a flight attendant began serving refreshments, so I laid the book aside.

Later, as I reached for my Bible again, I smiled. The yellow tag had come off the carry-on bag and was stuck to the leather covering. I was about to pull it off. But no! It seemed perfectly natural for those words to be displayed in such a prominent place.

To this day, that bright yellow sticker remains on the cover, so aptly describing what my Bible has become to me . . . SECURITY CHECK.

In so many ways the Bible assures me that the Lord is my real security.

> The LORD is . . . my fortress, and my deliverer . . . my rock, in whom I take refuge, my shield . . . my stronghold.
>
> (Psalm 18:2 RSV)

We have this hope [Christ] as an anchor for the
soul, firm and secure. (Hebrews 6:19 NIV)

You are my hiding place, you will save me from
trouble. (Psalm 32:7 TEV)

I will hide in God, who is my rock and my refuge
. . . and high tower. Thank you, O my Savior.
(2 Samuel 22:3 TLB)

For thou hast been a shelter for me, and a strong
tower from the enemy. (Psalm 61:3)

What pictures of SECURITY—fortress, deliverer,
rock, shield, hiding place, stronghold, refuge, anchor,
strong (and high) tower, shelter.

PRAYER:
Lord, what comfort, what peace is mine, when I put
myself under your divine protection. How I give
thanks for the hope I have in your security.

ᨘ *TODAY'S DELIGHT:*
*Do your own SECURITY CHECK with a concordance
by looking up references to the above words. To make
this word study even more fascinating, compare various
versions of the Bible.*

Dial Flipping

My husband is a TV dial flipper. Sometimes when I'm getting dinner, I hear something like this:

> Hold your fire and don't shoot until you're . . .
> At the fifty yard line. The quarterback is going
> to . . .
> Exercise mercy and deliberate with justice . . .
> When you taste just one bite of this crunchy
> cereal, filled with . . .
> Fabulous prizes, worth a million dollars . . .

You get the idea?

At that moment, the Western, football game, mystery drama, advertisements, and the game show are not holding his attention.

But when the posse is about to capture the desperadoes, when the jury is ready to announce its verdict, or especially when the team is on the goal line, he wouldn't dream of changing channels. At halftime, he may tell me about an exciting play or the latest score.

I often approach Bible reading in much the same way. I page flip, not concentrating on any one chapter or book of the Bible. But when I embark upon an in-depth study, I discover goals to strive for. As I get excited about God's Word, I want to share with others.

If you're new to Bible reading, start with a synoptic

Gospel (Matthew, Mark, Luke) or one of Paul's letters to the churches. Read the passages thoroughly, using available Bible helps. As biblical events and teachings become real, you'll have a sincere desire to tell others what you've learned.

🍃 *TODAY'S DELIGHT:*
As you watch TV today, do this: Instead of flipping to another channel during the ads, turn down the sound and repeat a Scripture you are memorizing, or offer a prayer to God.

A Helpful Device

I ran across an interesting word recently that, heretofore, was not in my vocabulary. Yet it pertains to something I've used for years. It's *mnemonics* (ni-mon-iks), a system for improving or developing one's memory.

The bit of trivia I read gave a couple examples of mnemonics: to learn the Great Lakes, for example, remember the word *HOMES*. That's "Huron, Ontario, Michigan, Erie, and Superior." Another example was this sentence, "My Very Educated Mother Just Served Us Nine Pickles." The initials will help you recite the planets in order: Mercury, Venus, Earth, Mars, Jupiter, Saturn, Uranus, Neptune, and Pluto.

Mnemonics were obviously employed when a retreat speaker once suggested a way to remember some of Paul's shorter epistles.

"Just think of General Electric Power Company," she said, "and you'll always remember Galatians, Ephesians, Philippians, and Colossians."

Later, for my own benefit, I added, "Followed by Five *T*s," and could rattle off "1 and 2 Thessalonians, 1 and 2 Timothy, and Titus."

I'd always had a struggle with the Minor Prophets, and came up with my own version of mnemonics. (Now, please don't laugh!)

> *Hosea Just Abhors Orange Juice.*
> *Micah Never Has.*
> *Zephaniah Hates [it].*
> *Zechariah May.*

Voilà! There you have Hosea, Joel, Amos, Obadiah, Jonah, Micah, Nahum, Habakkuk, Zephaniah, Haggai, Zechariah, Malachi.

You may ask, "How do you remember which 'J' prophet or which 'H' prophet comes first?" Easy! As long as I start my arrangement with Hosea, I then call to mind that alphabetically Habakkuk comes before Haggai, and Joel before Jonah. You may be quick to point out that the system breaks down with the "Z" prophets! Well, I didn't say my method was perfect!

My husband thinks it's crazy.

"It's just as hard to memorize your words as all those prophets' names," he claims. I pointed out to him it makes just as much sense as his childhood verse:

> *Matthew, Mark, Luke and John.*
> *Saddle the horse and I'll get on!*

Well, maybe his is a tad simpler!

❧ TODAY'S DELIGHT:
Create your own mnemonic formula for learning something biblical. If your mind does not click mnemonically (yes, that's a bona fide word!), check other memory helps on the next page.

Other Memory Tricks

*Thy word have I hid in mine heart, that I might
not sin against thee.* (Psalm 119:11)

Several years ago, our local retreat invited Florence
Turnidge as our speaker. Florence specializes in
teaching how to memorize God's Word.

She employs mnemonics, although she calls it
"Abbreviation." But she has several other memory
tricks to make the study of Scripture come alive. Here
are a few:

(1) *3 x 5 Cards*—Write out Scripture passages,
including the "address" (chapter and verse). Put
these cards in prominent places—on the bathroom mirror, above the kitchen sink, in your purse
or pocket. Recite verses while combing your hair
or during meal preparation. Repeat them when at a
stoplight or waiting in the dentist's office.

(2) *Association*—To learn Isaiah 26:3-4, for example, just remember that any twenty-six-year—old
woman with children, ages three and four, should
heed this advice. "Thou wilt keep him [her] in
perfect peace, whose mind is stayed on thee:
because he [she] trusteth in thee. Trust ye in the
LORD for ever: for in the LORD JEHOVAH is
everlasting strength" (KJV).

(3) *Word Pictures*—Florence relates, "When learning Psalm 100, I stumbled on verse four. Was it 'enter into his gates with thanksgiving, and into his courts with praise,' or the other way around? In my memory notebook, I drew a tiny turkey on top of a gate. Whenever I say the psalm, I visualize a Thanksgiving turkey perched upon a gate."

(4) *A Memory Partner*—Call this friend each week and recite your selections to each other. If you choose the same verse and discuss it, that Scripture will have a richer meaning to you both.

(5) *Group Participation*—Use your weekly verse for grace at mealtime or during family prayers. You'll be surprised how rapidly children will learn (they might even surpass you!). Begin a prayer group or church meeting with a verse that members have chosen to memorize.

(6) *Tape Recorder*—In learning a longer passage, record it on tape. Read slowly, pausing after a section so you can repeat it. Listen while driving, cleaning house, during an office lunch break.

(7) *Sing the Scriptures*—I have a list of over ninety Scriptures set to music. I underline these verses in a different color so they're easier to find. Or make up your own tunes. In either case, include the "address."

Florence told us about Madame Jeanne Guyon, a sixteenth-century saint, who suggested that a casual reading of the Bible is like a bee skimming the surface of a flower, but that praying the Scripture is like a bee penetrating into the blossom's depth to remove the nectar. Florence added, "Memorizing God's Word is like the bee taking the nectar home and making honey of it."

PRAYER:
Oh, Lord, I want to hide your Word in my heart. Block any thoughts that say I can't memorize it.

❧ *TODAY'S DELIGHT:*
Choose one of the above methods this very day and begin a program of memorization. Decide which seems best for you, but don't hesitate to try others as you begin to learn God's Word.

How? Ugh!

Surely goodness and mercy shall follow me all the days of my life. (Psalm 23:6)

For years, my husband always walked a few steps
   ahead of me.
We had a standing joke.
"How!" I'd call out to him. He would answer, "Ugh!"
(This was from Western movies in which the squaw
   trudged behind the chief!)
But I've noticed a change as we grow older.
Now I can actually hold his hand as we walk together.
Psalm 23 states that goodness and mercy shall *follow*
   us all the days of our lives.
Why *"follow"* us? Why not "shall walk side by side
   with us?" or "shall go before us"?
We've spent so many years—
   pursuing a career . . .
   raising a family . . .
   accumulating material goods . . .
that some of us have run ahead of the Lord.
But there's a nice thing about getting older.
Now we can slow down and let goodness and mercy
   catch up with us.

PRAYER:
Lord, how wonderful to know you're all encompass-
ing, and that you "hem [us] in—behind and before"
(Psalm 139:5 NIV).

❧ TODAY'S DELIGHT:
Go for a leisurely walk with your spouse or other
relative, a friend, or close neighbor. Stay in step with
each other, and if appropriate, hold hands.

Just the Facts, Ma'am!

This is the disciple who testifies to these things and who wrote them down. We know that his testimony is true.

My husband and I were on the highway one snowy January day. A speeding van full of young people passed us. The next day we read in the paper that a vehicle of that description had been involved in a fatal accident. We mentioned it to several friends, and as a result, word reached authorities, and we were called in as witnesses. We made a tape for the state patrol, had a deposition, and finally testified in court.

The attorney cautioned me, "Do not give your personal opinion, but just the facts, ma'am."

While on the witness stand, I said the van was traveling too fast for road conditions.

"Objection!" shouted the defense lawyer. That was my opinion. However, I *could* say the van fishtailed as it passed. That was a fact.

In his Gospel, John claims he has stated facts about his experiences with Christ. The theologian William Barclay says,

> John was the man who was able to say, "I saw these things, and I know that they are true." To this day the final argument for Christianity is Christian experience. To this day the Christian is

the man who can say, "I know Jesus Christ, and I know that these things are true."[1]

How often do I confuse opinion with fact—especially when it comes to my theological views? I've argued about biblical concepts, which later proved to be false.

In a sense, the Pharisees and other learned men in Jesus' day did much the same. They rigidly followed hundreds of man-made laws, confusing them with God's laws. Jesus plainly told the people, "Do not think that I have come to abolish the Law or the Prophets; I have not come to abolish them but to fulfill them" (Matthew 5:17 NIV).

My experiences with Christ are authentic, and I can testify to them. But in order to defend God's Word to a skeptic or share it with an honest seeker, I need to know what it says—and the only way I can know is to read and assimilate it. At the same time, I must not confuse opinion with fact so that I may be accountable to God, always speaking the truth.

PRAYER:
Lord, I want to be a witness to you and tell others what you have done in my life. But help me also to study your Word so that I can point the honest seeker to your truth.

[1] William Barclay, "The Gospel of John," in *The Daily Study Bible,* vol. 2 (Edinburgh: The Saint Andrew Press, 1965), 333.

Just the Facts, Ma'am!

❧ *TODAY'S DELIGHT:*
Is there something biblical about which you aren't sure?
Do a little research and seek out the answer in God's
Word. Use helpful tools such as a concordance, Bible
encyclopedia, dictionary, or a good commentary.

My Real Home

Jesus said: "If you make my word your home you will indeed be my disciples. (John 8:31, JB)

The most touching scene in the movie *E.T.*—for me, at least—was when the camera zoomed in on the extraterrestrial and he uttered the single word, "Home."

In a sense, we all have two homes—the physical surroundings in which we find ourselves and the emotional home in our minds. Those of us who find the two merged together are fortunate.

A pastor recently invited a couple to visit his church.

"Oh, we're not interested. You see, we don't know how long we'll be here." The couple had lived in town eight years! Emotionally, home was where they had lived before.

A touching epitaph appears on the Jamestown tombstone of a woman who, in 1619, came with others to marry lonely settlers.

"She touched the soil of Virginia with her little foot, and the wilderness became her home."

For most of us, "home" is where we receive sustenance, nurturing, and our values. It is a place where we find continuity in life. So it is altogether appropriate that John's statement, "if you continue in my word," be translated "make the word of God your home."

PRAYER:
Lord, I want to feel "at home"—at ease—in your Word. I want to know, without one doubt, that's where I belong—where I can receive spiritual sustenance and nurturing.

❧ *TODAY'S DELIGHT:*
Give a small donation to an organization that distributes Bibles or portions of Scripture to those who do not have access to God's Word.

Short But Significant

As thou hast sent me into the world, even so have I also sent them into the world.

(John 17:18)

Our pastor was preparing a sermon on missions when two little words in the above text jumped out at him. He decided to make those words the focal point in his message.

"*As* and *so*," began the pastor. "They are two of the shortest and most insignificant words in our language, but they are the key to missions in Christ's high priestly prayer."

He continued, "*As* the Father sent Jesus into the world to carry out his will—to feed the hungry, clothe the naked, heal the sick, and minister to the broken-hearted—*so* Jesus sent not only his disciples, but *so* he sends us."

Throughout the New Testament, we see the *as* and the *so* in Christ's life in action. *As* he taught his disciples how to meet the needs of the people, *so* he expected them to be involved.

The feeding of the five thousand is one example. *As* he showed love to those listening on that day, *so* he became an example to his followers.

The pastor's sermon prompted me to go further in studying these two seemingly insignificant words. I was surprised at my findings.

In the Gospels, I found Jesus' words to the centurion who asked that his servant be healed. *"As* thou hast believed, *so* be it done unto thee" (Matthew 8:13, emphasis mine). In John, I ran across these examples: "I do *as* the Father has commanded me, *so* that the world may know that I love the Father" (John 14:31 NRSV). In the next chapter, I found: *"As* the Father has loved me, *so* I have loved you" (John 15:9 NRSV).

Paul's letter to the Colossians has at least two great statements with these "insignificant" words. *"As* ye have therefore received Christ Jesus the Lord, *so* walk ye in him" (2:6); and, *"As* the Lord has forgiven you, *so* you also must forgive" (3:13 NRSV).

One other example I'd like to share: *"As* he is, *so* are we in this world" (1 John 4:17 NRSV).

Isn't that the heart of missions—that we represent him in this hurting world of ours? *As* and *so*—significant words, after all!

PRAYER:
Father, *as* you touch my life this day, *so* may I actively do your will.

☙ *TODAY'S DELIGHT:*
Look up all of the above verses in your Bible. Reading other versions often highlights a truth we need to know.

Two More Short Words

Then Manoah said, "Now when your words come true, what is to be the boy's rule of life; what is he to do?"
(Judges 13:12 NRSV)

Two more short but significant words caught my attention when reading through some of the darkest chapters in Scripture—in the book of Judges.

The thirteenth chapter relates the details surrounding the birth of Samson, one of Israel's judges.

It's difficult enough to imagine an angel appearing to a barren woman, telling her she will have a child. Can you further imagine her husband believing his wife and asking God to send the angel again in order to teach them how to bring up the child?

When the angel does return, the wife hurries to the field to get her husband. After making sure this is the heavenly visitor, Manoah asks, "If your words come true . . ." WAIT! Manoah does *not* ask, as would I, *"If* your words come true . . ."; rather, *"When* your words come true . . ." (emphasis mine).

After offering hospitality, Manoah then asks the visitor's name. In that request (13:17), we hear the same statement of faith, "What is your name, so that we may honor you *when* your words come true?" (emphasis mine).

Oh, that I could change my *if*s to *when*s! Not *"if* that

loved one would accept the Lord!" but *"when* that loved one accepts the Lord!" Not *"if* I could just lose an extra five pounds!" but *"when* I lose five pounds!"

What are the *if*s in your life? Can you stretch your faith to turn them into *when*s? Not *"if* I get the right job!" but *"when* I get the right job!" Not *"if* I can just finish this difficult project!" but *"when* I finish this difficult project!"

Try this small but significant change in your vocabulary. You'll like it!

PRAYER:
Lord, I need your guidance. I ask not *"if* you help me" but *"when* you help me . . ."* Thank you for your faithfulness.

❧ *TODAY'S DELIGHT:*
Make a conscious effort to watch your speech this day. Every time you find yourself making an if statement, change it to a when statement. Your faith will grow by leaps and bounds.

Straight Paths

"Swim for therapy," the doctor told me after shoulder surgery. I'd never cared much for the sport. No matter how careful I was, I bumped into other swimmers or the end of the pool.

Then I bought a pair of swim goggles. I concentrated on the lines painted on the pool's bottom, which enabled me to swim straight. I had to be more alert in deeper water as the lines grew dimmer. I watched for the painted cross lines at the end of the lane, signifying I had completed the lap and could rest a moment.

One day while I was swimming, a spiritual parallel occurred to me. When I concentrate on Christ's guidelines, I don't stray off the path. David asked the Lord, "Lead me . . . make your way straight before me" (Psalm 5:8 NRSV). So I also ask the Lord. Solomon advised, "Trust in the LORD with all your heart, and do not rely on your own insight. In all your ways acknowledge him, and he will make straight your paths" (Proverbs 3:5-6 NRSV). I too want to follow that advice. This is especially true when I'm in deep water and have lost my direction.

Likewise, by fixing my eyes on the Cross of Christ, I will attain the goals he sets for me and will find rest in him.

I discovered an added spiritual benefit as I swam. Counting laps became boring, so I began to memorize the books of the Bible. By mentally reciting the thirty-nine Old Testament books, I swam a little over a mile. I added an additional three-fourths mile to my swimming total by memorizing the twenty-seven New Testament books.

🍃 *TODAY'S DELIGHT:*
Turn a boring task into an opportunity to memorize the books of the Bible or Scripture verses (while riding a stationary bike, mowing the lawn, dusting, or waiting in a line of traffic).

A Divine Sleeping Pill

Casting down imaginations, and every high thing that exalteth itself against the knowledge of God, and bringing into captivity every thought to the obedience of Christ. (2 Corinthians 10:5)

"I used to be a good sleeper," my friend sighed. "But no more."
I don't know if we need less sleep as we grow older.
Or if we just have more aches and pains to keep us awake.
We follow all the advice we read about.
We cut down on the coffee.
We take a warm bath before retiring.
We may even forego the late news. Who wants to dream of world events?
Do you remember, as I do, nights you used to lie awake waiting for a loved one to get home? (Perhaps you still do.)
Or how you worried about the office, the lab, the classroom?
One of my children provided an ideal scenario for sleepless nights.
That's when I discovered a divine sleeping pill . . . 2 Corinthians 10:5.
I memorized the Phillips version, "We fight to capture

215

every thought until it acknowledges the authority of
Christ."
And fight I did!
As I put the skids on my imagination . . .
As I mentally forced my negative thoughts to obey
Christ.
This same remedy works today, during those
sleepless nights when I worry about my energy
level, my health, and my grandchildren.
May I suggest you switch prescriptions?
You won't find a better divine sleeping aid.
But like any medication, it must be followed faithfully
for the best results.

PRAYER:
Help me to "cast down" my vivid imagination, Lord,
and bring every thought captive to your authority.

&• *TODAY'S DELIGHT:*
*Look forward to the luxury of a warm bubble bath before
retiring tonight. You men might even enjoy one!*

Delight in Oneself

If my religion's not all
That it ought to be.
The trouble's not with God,
The trouble's with me.

—Anonymous

This above all: to thine own self
  be true,
And it must follow, as the night
  the day,
Thou canst not then be false
  to any man.

—William Shakespeare
(1564–1616), *Hamlet*

Don't Look Back!

The one thing I do . . . is to forget what is behind me and do my best to reach what is ahead.

(Philippians 3:13 TEV)

My husband and I were taking our first bike ride of the season. After years of biking, I still feel like a beginner on my first outing each spring.

Approaching an intersection, I heard a car behind me. I glanced back. My bike veered to the right, and the wheel scraped the curbing. Over I went. Luckily, my only damage was a skinned knee, a broken fingernail, and total embarrassment.

"What happened?" Kyle asked.

I meekly replied, "I looked back."

It's so easy to look back on past mistakes, such as those I made while raising my children. And when an older relative criticized my maternal efforts, anger hitchhiked along with guilt. For years, these destructive emotions kept me from a closer walk with God.

What a lesson Paul teaches me! He refused to dwell on past ugly mistakes or unfair criticism. He put those things behind him, and kept his eye on what was ahead, wanting to "run straight toward the goal in order to win the prize, which is God's call through Christ Jesus to the life above" (3:14 TEV).

Don't Look Back!

Lord, I want to follow Paul's footsteps on my spiritual journey. Help me to focus on this day, not bound by past mistakes or fear of the future. Thanks, dear Father.

  🕊 *TODAY'S DELIGHT:*
If the weather warrants it, take a bike ride. Wear a bike helmet for safety. Or go for a walk, on the proper side of the road (facing oncoming traffic).

Who Sabotaged My Body?

> *"But I will restore you to health and heal your wounds,"* declares the LORD.　　　(Jeremiah 30:17 NIV)

Who sabotaged my body? This frame was a good friend, but lately it acts like an enemy.

Then I'm reminded of:

Robert Louis Stevenson . . . who declared, while traveling around the world searching for the right environment for his damaged lungs, "I am made of the stuff soldiers are made from, but God willed it that my battle should be one with medicine bottles and pill boxes."

Amy Carmichael . . . who wrote prolifically during twenty years of illness. She stated that things written by those in pain helped a reader as nothing except the words of Jesus could do!

Anne Ortlund . . . a contemporary writer, who started her book *The Disciplines of the Beautiful Woman* the second day after surgery. She wrote: "How silly of me to give God only my heart . . . and not my body! . . . I am absolutely relaxed to let him do what he wants. . . . Pain is God's beautiful gift to make us lean harder on him, when he knows we need it."[1]

God has often restored my health and healed my

[1] Anne Ortlund, *The Disciplines of the Beautiful Woman* (Waco, Tex.: Word Books, 1977), 10-11. Used by permission.

wounds. Sometimes not. I don't know why, but I leave that up to him.

My part is to refuse to dwell on my aches and pains.

PRAYER:
Lord, as my spirit communes with thy Spirit, I also turn my body over to you.

ҙ *TODAY'S DELIGHT:*
If you've been putting off an appointment to the doctor or dentist, make one today. It will be a delight to get those teeth—or that body—tended to!

Sharp Barbs—Year-Round!

Do not use harmful words in talking. Use only helpful words, the kind that build up and provide what is needed, so that what you say will do good to those who hear you. (Ephesians 4:29 TEV)

One August morning I sat on the davenport reading the paper. My foot hit something sharp as I rubbed my bare sole over the carpet.

Reaching down among the strands of the deep shag, I was amazed to find a Christmas tree ornament hanger.

In August? It had apparently been buried there since December! I'd walked barefoot over that spot often. I'd vacuumed weekly, not counting a few extra runs before entertaining company.

Fortunately, the ornament hanger did no damage to my foot, but its very existence in the carpet for eight months caused me to ponder.

Perhaps there are sharp barbs of unforgiveness and bitterness buried in my subconscious. Would they eventually work themselves to the surface at a time when least expected? Would they "puncture" or hurt some innocent person?

I confess my judgmental thoughts often become words with harmful thorns of sarcasm and criticism, or actions for which I am later ashamed.

I obviously need to improve my housecleaning skills and do a more thorough job of vacuuming. But more than that, I need to do a better job of housecleaning my mind, not just for "special occasions," but as a daily checkup so that my words may edify and impart grace. (See Ephesians 4:29 in the King James Version.)

PRAYER:
Lord, teach me to say only what is good and helpful to those I talk to, and what will give them a blessing. (See Ephesians 4:29 in *The Living Bible.)*

à *TODAY'S DELIGHT:*
If you know the ancient Hebrew folk song "King of Kings and Lord of Lords,"[1] *glory, hallelujah! Sing it while you vacuum. You'll actually enjoy the task! (Men, you can run a vacuum too!)*

---

[1] "King of Kings," Sophie Conty and Naomi Batya (*Music Net*™ Maranatha! Music, 1980).

Ha Ha! Hee Hee! Ho Ho!

A merry heart doeth good like a medicine.

(Proverbs 17:22)

Ha Ha! Hee Hee! Ho Ho! Go ahead and laugh, Shirley! It's better than ibuprofen or aspirin! It releases endorphins in your system.

Releases what?

I'd been collecting articles on laughter and health, humor and well-being for a long time. I dug through my "Positive Emotions" file and found titles such as:

"Power of Laughter Taken Seriously"
"Laughter Is Good Medicine"
"Ailing? Take Two Jokes and . . ."
"Laugh and Feel Better"
"Laughter Good for Health, Both Emotional,
    Physical"
"Take Time to Laugh"
"A Prescription for Humor"

Some of the articles dated back over ten years to when Norman Cousins's book, *The Anatomy of an Illness*, told of his self-prescribed program of focusing on positive emotions and using laughter in the healing process.

One study written in an American Association of Retired Persons news bulletin told of folks in a

Georgia hospital receiving an unusual prescription: a few hours in a humor room. Devoid of medical equipment, this room was stocked with videotapes of old movies of Laurel and Hardy, W. C. Fields, reruns of "Candid Camera," and classic radio shows featuring Red Skelton, Groucho Marx, Abbott and Costello, and Amos 'n' Andy.

They found that laughter eased muscular tension, helped the respiratory system, and increased oxygen in the blood. In other words, laughter *was* good exercise.

An article in a leading women's magazine suggested ways to laugh oneself to better health—ideas such as keeping a humor first-aid kit stocked with cartoons, jokes, and comedy tapes. Or brightening up a room with cheerful posters, wacky bumper stickers, and zany signs. The author suggested scheduling a ten-minute "humor break" every day.

One well-known punster and director of a humor project put it this way, "People should avoid hardening of the attitudes."

It's "all in your head" in a physiological sense as well. When you laugh, the body's immune system is stimulated and endorphins are released. These natural hormonelike substances with painkilling and tranquilizing properties are secreted by the brain.

You didn't forget a thing in creating this body, did you, God?

PRAYER:
Thank you, Lord, for your divine blueprint. Thank you for giving me the ability to laugh.

&❧ *TODAY'S DELIGHT:*
Check your television schedule for a sidesplitting comedy. Or rent a video of one of the comedy teams of yesteryear. And laugh until your sides hurt!

God's Medicine

A merry heart maketh a cheerful countenance.

(Proverbs 15:13)

The other day my aerobics teacher told us that smiles are somehow connected with hormones from the pituitary gland. When you smile, she said, this gland is stimulated and elevates one's mood.

There wasn't much to smile about when I was a youngster during the depression. But I still remember a poem my mother taught me that went something like this:

> *Smile and the world smiles with you.*
> *Kick and you kick alone.*
> *For the cheerful grin will let you in*
> *Where the kicker is never known.*

I tried to find the source of this poem and discovered similar words in "Solitude" by Ella Wheeler Wilcox, written sometime after the Civil War:

> *Laugh and the world laughs with you.*
> *Weep and you weep alone.*
> *For the sad old earth must borrow its mirth,*
> *But has trouble enough of its own.*

The nineteenth century preacher Henry Ward Beecher called mirth God's medicine. He said, "Everybody ought to bathe in it. Grim care, moroseness, anxiety—all this rust of life ought to be scoured off by the oil of mirth. It is better than emery. Every man ought to rub himself with it."[1]

PRAYER:
God, help me to take a big dose of your medicine this day. Your Word tells me that a happy heart will make my face cheerful.

≈▲ *TODAY'S DELIGHT:*
Stand in front of the mirror and smile at yourself. Then pass that smile on to the people who come into your life today.

---

[1] Charles L. Wallis, *Words of Life* (New York: Harper & Row, Publishers, 1966), 203.

First Things First

Those that seek me early shall find me.

(Proverbs 8:17)

"Is it the maid's day off?"

When I was first married and failed to make the bed, my husband always jokingly asked this question. He could ignore a sink full of dirty dishes, an unkempt living room, but he always noticed an unmade bed. So for the first thirty years of marriage, I tried to make the bed as soon as I got up.

One day I failed to do this morning ritual. I became engrossed in a writing project and spent several hours at my typewriter. My creativity was interrupted by a voice.

"Mom, I'm home. And guess who's here?"

My daughter, home for the summer, caught me off guard. A college boyfriend dropped by unexpectedly, and her boss had graciously allowed her to leave work early.

After introductions and small talk, I returned to my typewriter in time to hear Laurie say, "That's Mom's office, and this is the folks' bedroom. Oops! I guess Mom forgot to make the bed!"

I'm sure the young man had seen unmade beds before, but I felt guilty. I had not expected company, and, of all days, wondered why I'd broken my bed-making habit.

I also try to spend time each day with the Lord, reading his Word and praying. But sometimes I put other things first. Sure enough, I feel guilty and the day doesn't go as well when I leave him out of it. When the something unforeseen crops up, I'm unprepared to deal with it.

By the way, since retirement, my husband has taken over the bed-making chore and does a better job than I! But no one else can take over my job of communing with the Lord on a daily basis.

PRAYER:
Help me to establish the habit of seeking you early in the day, Lord.

&· *TODAY'S DELIGHT:*
Make your bed with joy, thanking God for a good night's sleep and the comfort provided. (If you've already completed that task, plan to do this for the next few days.)

Betrayal

All of them deserted him and fled. (Mark 14:50 NRSV)

The fellowship was warm as we shared what God had been doing for us that week. I left the prayer meeting determined to tell everyone about our precious Lord.

On the way home I stopped at a store. As I stood in the checkout line, two shabbily dressed women were discussing a local church's bus ministry. Their comments were disparaging. Some of the folks involved in this outreach work were in my prayer group. I knew their work resulted in youngsters from poorer areas of town being able to attend Sunday school.

One of the women said loudly, "Why don't they stick to their own neighborhoods and leave us alone?" Then, turning to me, she added contemptuously, "Ain't it an awful waste of gas?"

Embarrassed, I turned my head and pretended to study a magazine on a nearby rack. As I returned home, I knew I had betrayed my Lord, the one with whom I had spent such sweet communion an hour before, the one whose message of love I had so wanted to share.

PRAYER:
Lord, forgive me when I desert you. Give me the boldness to speak out for you in love, so that I may once again "delight in myself."

232

🕊 *TODAY'S DELIGHT:*
Check with your church to see if there are youngsters in
your area who need a ride to Sunday school. If possible,
arrange transportation. Or help financially to support
an ongoing bus ministry.

First appeared in *The Quiet Hour,* June 25, 1982.

Can You "Flunk" Church?

How great is the love the Father has lavished on us, that we should be called children of God! And that is what we are!   (1 John 3:1 NIV)

After attending seminary in America, a young Kenyan woman returned to her home country and was assigned to a new church. She diligently called upon people in the surrounding villages and countryside until the membership rose from three to three hundred members.

One parishioner yearned for her husband to attend church. The woman pastor went into the fields and helped the man tend his cattle. After many visits, she invited him to attend worship services.

"I can't. I flunked church."

Curious, the pastor asked how.

"Once I took a confirmation test. They asked me who first saw Jesus after he was resurrected."

"What did you answer?"

"I said the animals. So I flunked church."

"You cannot flunk church," the pastor explained. "And you cannot flunk God." She then told the Kenyan farmer of God's everlasting love for him.

Do you feel like you've "flunked" church? When you received a cold welcome at a place of worship? Or suffered embarrassment when you took a stand on an ethical issue? Did someone scoff at your interpretation of a Scripture or your form of worship?

Here's wonderful news! You haven't flunked church or God. You're his child and he loves you!

PRAYER:
Lord, thank you for your unconditional love. May I never be a stumbling block to an honest seeker.

🍃 *TODAY'S DELIGHT:*
Place a small cement block or a child's block in a conspicuous place. Let it remind you never to be a stumbling block to another.

Does Your Christianity Leak?

The joy of the LORD is your strength.

I'm not very happy.

I'm growing older, and I don't like it one bit.

All I want is just a little happiness in my latter years!

And, oh yes, joy too!

Then I look at those words—*happy*—*joy*.

Happy—from Middle English *hap*—occurrence,
    fortune, chance.

Joy—from Vulgar Latin *gaudia*—unattested, delight,
    rejoice.

I can be UNhappy when things go wrong. But UNjoy?
    Impossible!

When I focus on circumstances, I am either happy or
    unhappy.

But when I focus on the Lord, I experience a joy
    beyond the most difficult circumstances.

The word *JOY* forms an acronym:

    J—Jesus,

    O—Others,

    Y—You

When relationships come in that order, joy is the
    by-product.

The well-known evangelist Billy Sunday once said,

"If you have no joy in your religion,

there's a leak in your Christianity."

PRAYER:
Lord, help me plug up the holes in my religion so the joy won't leak.

&c *TODAY'S DELIGHT:*
Find an old plug or cork. Put it in a conspicuous place—on the windowsill, your desk, or your bed stand. Let it remind you that "the joy of the Lord is your strength."

Second Fiddle

Do business with these until I come back.

(Luke 19:13 NRSV)

I was delighted! I'd been asked to speak at a women's retreat, quite an honor considering the size of the gathering. I did wonder why they waited so long to ask, but no matter. Then one of the ladies let it slip. At the last minute, a nationally known Christian speaker had canceled. I was second choice!

Conflicting emotions swept over me. *How can I ever fill her shoes? On the other hand, I should be proud! But, then again—second fiddle . . . ?*

Ironically, I'd just read a story about Leontyne Price, the famous American soprano, who played "second fiddle" after the leading lady in the opera *Aida* suffered an appendectomy. A year later, the same thing happened in London. Miss Price said her career was launched on the "appendectomies of Italian sopranos." She was so well prepared she eventually sang *Aida* at Milan's La Scala without a rehearsal.

The same article told of Oscar Hammerstein, who had experienced eleven years of failure when he was asked to play second fiddle to the brilliant Lorenz Hart. Richard Rodgers contacted him, explaining that Hart was opposed to a new dual assignment. Rodgers was reluctant to proceed without Hart, but had a family and career to consider, whereas Hammerstein hesitated about replacing a partner of such long standing. But he finally agreed, and thus was born the historic partnership of Rodgers and Hammerstein, starting with the classic *Oklahoma*, all because the latter was willing to be second fiddle.

I thought of my children's school band days. As second or third chair, they had the opportunity to challenge the first chair. They rehearsed diligently, hoping to make it to that top spot. In the meantime, they kept playing "second fiddle" to the best of their ability to be ready for the next "challenge day."

During their "off" times, both Price and Hammerstein kept themselves prepared. They knew that "second fiddles" ("understudies" in the world of music and theater) must be just as good as the star being replaced.

I had material at my fingertips on which to speak, so I could accept the last-minute invitation. And what a blessing I received! I'm convinced we need to keep those talents God has given each of us in readiness for his use when he calls upon us. He wants us to "do business" with what he has given us until his return.

PRAYER:
Lord, thank you for the gifts you've given me; the gifts of _____, _____, and _____. May I always use these talents for your glory. Amen.

Second Fiddle

Two Games

I will restore to you the years which the swarming
locust has eaten, the hopper, the destroyer, and the
cutter. . . . You shall . . . praise the name of the
LORD your God, who has dealt wondrously with you.

When I have nothing better to do, I play two games.
The "if only" game with the past and the "what if"
    game with the future.
Sometimes I change the rules of the "what if" game.
I choose to stop worrying about the greenhouse
    effect on the earth . . .
    the unrest in the Middle East . . .
    my own mortality . . .
But change the "if only" game rules? Impossible!
If only I'd tried harder to understand my mother . . .
If only I'd started my career sooner . . .
If only I'd disciplined my children differently . . .
Mercifully, God has rewritten the "if only" rules.
He will restore the years eaten by the swarming
    locusts of failure . . .
    the hopper of self-pity . . .
    the destroyer of pride . . .
    the cutter of unkind remarks.
He not only heals my past mistakes, but he forgets
    them too!
So can I!

PRAYER:
"Restore us to yourself, O LORD, that we may be restored . . ." (Lamentations 5:21 NRSV).

🌸 *TODAY'S DELIGHT:*
Write on a 3 x 5 card, "You will trample our sins underfoot and send them to the bottom of the sea" (Micah 7:19 TEV). Then print: "NO FISHING ALLOWED."

P.S. Hide that mental fishing rod and net!

Gray-Haired Old Lady

*I will be your God through all your lifetime, yes,
even when your hair is white with age. I made you
and I will care for you. I will carry you along and
be your Savior.* (Isaiah 46:4 TLB)

I wasn't prepared for it. Yet I heard him call me a
"gray-haired old lady."

My mirror told me a different story, but that's how I
must have appeared to him. I was angry and hurt.
Then I took a long hard look at the name caller. He
wasn't a teenager, or a young adult—in fact, he was
probably fifteen or twenty years my senior! That's
when I started to laugh!

Few things are as relative as one's age. When you
turn thirty, your youngster tells his playmates that
Dad is sure getting old. On the other hand, my
octogenarian friend refers to sixty-year-olds as
"young."

Someone once made the remark, "You don't grow
old; you grow more so." Come to think of it, I've
known some very "young" seventy-year-olds, as well
as a few thirty-year-olds whose judgmental and
opinionated outlook made them seem ancient!

Samuel Ullman wrote a good description of age.
"Nobody grows old merely by a number of years. We
grow old by deserting our ideals . . . you are as young

243

as your faith, as old as your doubt; as young as your self-confidence, as old as your fear; as young as your hope, as old as your despair."[1]

A positive, cheerful outlook will turn you into a positive, cheerful older person. If you're critical, morose, no fun to be around, you'll grow into . . . well, you get my point.

So next time you see a "gray-haired old lady" or a "bald-headed old man," just remember that inside his or her body may be a mind, soul, and spirit far younger than your own!

PRAYER:
How comforting, Lord, to have your promise that, no matter what my age, you will care for me and carry me along.

&❧ *TODAY'S DELIGHT:*
Contact an older friend and give him or her a "warm fuzzy." It might be in the form of a compliment, a "thinking of you" card, anything that will make your friend feel years younger.

---

[1] Charles L. Wallis, ed., *The Treasure Chest* (New York: Harper & Row, Publishers, 1965), 11.

Wrinkles

Some things haven't changed since the early 1500s when Ponce de Leon searched for the legendary Fountain of Youth. The Spanish explorer drank water from every spring he came upon while exploring Florida, hoping to discover the marvelous fountain that could reputedly restore one's youth.

Nowadays folks may not drink from springs; rather, they're turning to facelifts and every imaginable cream and lotion. A deluge of articles have appeared the last couple of years: "Science Takes the Wrinkles Out of Aging," "Anti-Wrinkle Hope," "Yes, You Can Erase Wrinkles," "The Magic No-More-Wrinkles Cream." Stores have been besieged with requests for this irresistible product—Retin-A.

Let's face it—none of us wants to look older. But I was struck by a comment from a professor of dermatology: "In order to get wrinkles, you must have muscle action. If you never used your muscles, if you were blind all your life and never went in the sun, if you drank through a straw and never expressed anything, you'd have absolutely beautiful skin at ninety-two without wrinkles."[1]

Although you may create a future wrinkle each time

[1] Stephen Rae, "Wrapping the Human Package," *Modern Maturity,* June/July 1991, 91. He added that women normally have more wrinkles because they are more facially expressive than men.

Wrinkles

you smile, I agree with Samuel Ullman's observation, "Years wrinkle the skin, but to give up enthusiasm wrinkles the soul."

Let's be satisfied with ourselves, growing old gracefully, smiling all the while.

❧ *TODAY'S DELIGHT:*
Today when you apply face cream or shaving lotion, look in the mirror and reward yourself with a big smile. Then plan to smile at everyone you meet today.

Delight in Nature

Doth not all nature around me praise God? If I were silent, I should be an exception to the universe. Doth not the thunder praise Him as it rolls like drums in the march of the God of armies? Do not the mountains praise Him when the woods upon their summits wave in adoration? Does not the lightning write His name in letters of fire? Hath not the whole earth a voice? And shall I, can I, silent be?

—Charles H. Spurgeon
(1834–1892)

And nature, the old nurse, took
The child upon her knee.
Saying, "Here is a story book
My father hath writ for thee.
Come, wander with me," she said.
"In regions yet untrod
And read what is still unread
In the manuscripts of God."

—Henry Wadsworth Longfellow
(1807–1882)

Daffodils

For, lo, the winter is past, the rain is over and gone; the flowers appear on the earth.

(Song of Solomon 2:11-12)

A few moments ago I gazed out of my office window, wondering what to write about today. We're having an early spring, and the season's flowers are all in bloom. A cluster of yellow catches my eye—daffodils. They immediately remind me of another early spring day.

We'd taken the family for a Sunday afternoon outing in the mountains where winter still reigned. Yet here in the valley, spring had arrived.

That Monday morning the house was a mess. Dirty dishes were stacked on the table, the living room was in disarray, boots and gloves were strewn about from the snow trip. I couldn't seem to shift into high gear.

About then, my five-year-old son, who had been playing outside, came bursting in, a daffodil in his fists.

"Mommy, may I pick this yellow flower?" His enthusiasm had surpassed the family rule of getting permission before picking. Carefully examining the blossom, he began to ask other questions. With the help of an encyclopedia, I came up with answers.

"This is the stamen, the pistil (no, not the kind you shoot!), the pollen." He was fascinated as I told him how a bee gets the "yellow dust" on its feet and flies to another flower.

Daffodils

"Did you ever write a poem about daffodils?" he asked. (At that time, I wrote for children.)

"No, but somebody else did." I searched until I found a book of poetry containing Wordsworth's poem "Daffodils."

> *I wandered lonely as a cloud*
> *That floats on high o'er vales and hills,*
> *When all at once I saw a crowd,*
> *A host of golden daffodils;*
> *Beside the lake, beneath the trees,*
> *Fluttering and dancing in the breeze.*

Steve jumped up and began to "flutter" and "dance" around the room. We both laughed and I continued reading, ending with those memorable words:

> *And then my heart with pleasure fills,*
> *And dances with the daffodils.*

An hour later the house was still in a mess. The dirty dishes still covered the table. The boots and gloves reminded me of our wonderful family outing. Both mountain and valley showed tangible signs of God's creative power. How grateful I was that I'd taken the time to share God's beauty with my child.

That was twenty-five years ago; yet the daffodils still bloom in my yard, bringing back precious memories. And I continue to say with the bard of old, " . . . my heart with pleasure fills, and dances with the daffodils."

PRAYER:
Thank you, Lord, for creating flowers for our enjoyment. Prepare my heart for unexpected moments to see your handiwork through the eyes of a child.

❧ *TODAY'S DELIGHT:*
Pick a flower from your garden. Or buy a single bloom at your supermarket or florist. Examine it carefully; note its intricacies; thank God for making that blossom.

Consider the Ant

Take a lesson from the ants, you lazy fellow. Learn from their ways and be wise! (Proverbs 6:6 TLB)

On a warm May day, it's fun to lie on one's stomach and watch an ant carrying a load many times its own size—or to observe the activity in an anthill. I'm amazed at their industrious nature and remember the admonition in the Proverbs passage above.

Negative ant "behavior" can also teach us valuable lessons. Many ant colonies are headed by a queen ant, who spends her life laying eggs. Without this queen producing new offspring, all hope is gone for that ant colony.

That's what happened a couple of years ago at our national zoo, when worker ants of a leaf-cutting colony inadvertently beheaded their queen. Perhaps they tried to get her through a hole that was too small for the queen's head.

A newspaper editorial entitled "'Oops' in the Ant World," suggested that "lest we scoff at the stupidity of the leaf-cutters, ponder a bit. Like the industrious ants, we too may think our actions are for the best. Yet we remain blind to deadly consequences as plain to others as that headless creature is, to us, plainly dead."

How often I've thought my course of action was by

far the best way to tackle a problem. And how often I've been wrong!

I'm so grateful there is a "King" in my "colony" who not only produces new "spiritual" offspring but also will overlook the stupid actions of his "workers."

And the best news of all—this King will never die!

PRAYER:
Father, thank you for the valuable lessons I can learn from studying your wonderful world of nature.

🐦 *TODAY'S DELIGHT:*
If the weather warrants it, watch ants in your yard. Or study one of God's other creatures.

Up from the Ashes

I remember that Sunday morning vividly—May 18, 1980. Just before the church service ended, the sanctuary grew eerily dark. My husband whispered to me, "Quite a storm brewing outside!"

Within a half hour of returning home, we learned the truth. Mount St. Helens, in the southwestern part of our state, had erupted. Six hundred million tons of dust and ash spewed into the atmosphere, paralyzing cities more than three hundred miles away. Our town was not in the direct path of the blowing ash, due to the wind direction that day. Other communities to the north and east of us were not so lucky. Over 800,000 tons of gray ash fell within the city limits of Yakima alone! It was so heavy roofs collapsed, axles of dump trucks broke under the weight. The powderlike substance played havoc with car engines and people's lungs.

The force of the explosion was equivalent to more than twenty thousand Hiroshima-sized bombs! Fifty-seven people lost their lives. Two hundred thirty square miles of lush forests were blasted into stark barrenness; in fact, trees two hundred feet long and six feet in diameter were tumbled like matchsticks. Unleashed mudflows disrupted ship traffic some sixty miles downstream in the Columbia River.

How could any good come from such devastation? And yet . . .

Scientists claim that without volcanoes, life on earth as we know it would disappear! The heat beneath the earth's surface keeps erosion in check so that the world won't slip below sea level. Carbon-based life forms—from flowers to fish to humans—would become extinct.

In our farming area, volcanoes have been responsible for mineral-enriched soils, while in other parts of the world, valuable metals—gold, copper, even diamonds—have been produced by volcanic forces.

Survivors saw no good that May morning. One commented, "You work a lifetime to have a nice home and possessions, and it's wiped out in a flash."

Another added, "It took five minutes. We lost all our furniture and clothes. It was awful." She held up a teakettle, all that remained from a $100,000 dream house.

I keep a jar filled with Mount St. Helens's volcanic ash on my desk. When I look at it, I ask myself, what are *my* priorities? Do I put my trust in material possessions, in my intellect, my talents? If these things were suddenly taken away, could I trust God to bring good from the loss?

He promises to give me "beauty for ashes" (Isaiah 61:3 TLB) as I make a conscious decision to trust him with the circumstances of my life.

&▲ *TODAY'S DELIGHT:*
Take a glass jar and place some symbol of your security in it—a stub from your paycheck; dirt from your property; a key to your home; a medal or blue ribbon you've

255

won; a memento made by one of your children or grandchildren. Let the item remind you that neither money, material possessions, or people are your real security—only the true God.

Daylight Savings Time—What Do We Save?

I've often wondered how people from bygone days managed their daylight hours. Would they laugh at our daylight savings time?

There is just so much daylight in any given twenty-four hours. I'm not sure what we *save,* but there are some things we *lose* from this time manipulation.

Tempers, for instance. Do you remember when your kids equated bedtime with darkness? I would often *lose* my temper, trying to get the kids to bed at a decent hour.

"But, Mom, all the other guys stay outside until dark." Or, "I have to go to bed earlier than any kid in the neighborhood."

It wasn't so bad after the school year ended, except nobody wanted to eat supper until seven or eight o'clock. Any diet-conscious person knows it's difficult to *lose* those extra pounds eating a heavy meal so close to bedtime.

I *lose* precious hours of reading. Curling up with a book is my after-dark pastime. When it's daylight, I feel obliged to continue my labor. People who work in offices or factories all day appreciate the extra hour for yard work. I hate to admit it, but that's a chore I avoid zealously. The sooner it gets dark, the sooner I *lose* sight of those noxious weeds.

There are also initial mix-ups as we "spring ahead" and "fall back." Our oldest daughter was married the last Sunday in April. Some folks arrived at the church in time for a glass of punch and a piece of wedding cake. The process is reversed in the fall. We get to church an hour early and wonder where everybody else is.

"Fast" time or "slow" time, spring or fall, the psalmist hit the nail on the head when he said, "My times are in your hands" (Psalm 31:15 NIV).

🍂 *TODAY'S DELIGHT:*
Do something special with a loved one during the "extra" hour of daylight. If you're reading this in the winter, curl up with a good book during those dark hours after supper. (Stay away from the TV tonight!)

Morning Glory and Sin

And the blood of Jesus his Son cleanses us from all sin. (1 John 1:7 NRSV)

I have a confession to make. I hate to garden! Oh, I love a nice-looking yard, but I'd rather take a beating than work in it. I've partially solved the problem by hiring a young couple with a landscape business. I'm helping them get a start in their new venture, and at the same time, keeping my frustration level at a minimum.

However, I ran out of money for regular maintenance and was forced to do the weeding myself. Our corner lot is bordered on two sides by streets; the yard behind us looks like a page out of *Better Homes and Gardens*; the fourth side is an elementary school parking lot, with about ten feet of grass—and weeds—separating us.

The other day I decided to tackle the wild morning glory growing on the school lot. It had twisted and twined through the chain link fence that divides our property and was beginning to cover our Scotch pine trees as well as choking out flowers planted along the fence. The job seemed insurmountable! The pesky morning glory was impervious to most weed killers on the market, and I couldn't dig down ten to twelve feet to the source of the roots.

As I kept pulling and digging, I sensed the Lord trying to tell me something.

"Shirley, this morning glory is like sin in your life. It has gained a persistent foothold and threatens to choke out the beauty I've placed within you."

I changed the subject as I spoke aloud, "God, it's just not fair! The morning glory is on school property; yet I'm the one who has to deal with it." But God brought me back to the issue at hand.

"Others have often had to deal with the results of your sin, my child." Why did I suddenly recall those times when I'd spoken an unkind word or acted in a selfish manner?

I leaned up against the chain link fence and silently asked, "Lord, it's hopeless! If my sins are like the morning glory, they can't be eradicated!"

"Don't compare commercial weed killers with the blood of my only Son. You need only ask, and his blood will cleanse you from *all* sin."

PRAYER:
Lord, I come to you this day, asking forgiveness for my sins, and accepting the sacrifice Jesus made for me on the cross.

&. *TODAY'S DELIGHT:*
Get out in your garden and do a thorough weeding. If you have no garden, or if it's winter, "weed" out that messy closet, cupboard, or desk drawer that has been

accumulating junk. With each weed pulled or item discarded, ask God to help you "pull up" or "throw out" a bad habit that has prevented you from becoming the person he wants you to be.

Turbulence

Had I never flown before, I'd have been scared to death! The eighteen-passenger commuter plane was being buffeted mercilessly. Something like this might not have surprised me during a raging winter storm, but it was a bright sunny day, with unlimited visibility.

To get my mind off the turbulence, I pulled out a brochure from the pocket in front of me. It contained a list of questions that passengers ask. I began reading: "In warm weather, descent may be accompanied by bumpiness, by thermals (convective air currents), or by wind flowing over mountainous terrain. At this point, passengers will want to make sure their seat belts are securely fastened and carry-on items are placed under the seat in front of them." We *had* just flown over the Cascade Range, and the temperature on the ground below registered over 100 degrees! No wonder we felt bumps!

Pilots are taught how to fly in every kind of weather and are keenly aware that turbulence comes in all sizes from little choppiness to big, hard clouts. It affects the plane near the ground and up high where jets fly.

A few minutes later, our pilot explained the phenomenon over the intercom. I relaxed, knowing I was in good hands.

It's not unusual for me to experience emotional and spiritual bumps on my faith walk. I often fret and worry, until I remember a place to look for help. I pick up the Book that contains answers to the problems confronting me.

Likewise, my problems come in all shapes and sizes, affecting me wherever I am. I can learn to weather the storms of life when I put myself into the hands of my loving Pilot.

❧ *TODAY'S DELIGHT:*
Memorize these words to an old German hymn written by Paul Gerhardt in 1653 and translated by John Wesley in 1739:

> *Give to the winds thy fears;*
> *Hope and be undismayed;*
> *God hears thy sighs and counts thy tears,*
> *God shall lift up thy head.*
>
> *Through waves and clouds and storms,*
> *He gently clears thy way;*
> *Wait thou his time; so shall this night*
> *Soon end in joyous day.*[1]

[1] From *The Methodist Hymnal* (Board of Education of The Methodist Church, Inc., 1989), #129, verses 1 and 2.

October Days

October is transition time in our part of the country. It's a time when we must shift gears—from windbreakers and light sweaters to heavy jackets and coats, from air-conditioning units in our cars to the antifreeze in our radiators, from mowing grass to raking leaves.

The leaves remind me of a poem by George Cooper, titled *October's Party*.

> *October gave a party*
> *The leaves by hundreds came,*
> *The Chestnuts, Oaks and Maples,*
> *And leaves of every name . . .*
>
> *The Chestnuts came in yellow,*
> *The Oaks in crimson dressed,*
> *The lovely Misses Maples*
> *In scarlet looked their best.*

The poem talks about "Miss Weather" leading the dancing while "Professor Wind" leads the band. On days when "Professor Wind" whips up the colorful leaves, we can almost imagine a round dance in progress, led by "Miss Weather."

It would be wonderful if we could fill our mind and heart with October's beauty for the gray winter days that follow. But even when captured on canvas or in a poem, each autumn is different from the one that preceded it.

October, I apologize when I complain about your drizzly overcast days and your early morning hints of winter. I thank you for your colorful beauty, your Indian summer days, and your bountiful harvests.

ᲔᲮ *TODAY'S DELIGHT:*
Press some colorful fall leaves between the covers of a heavy book.

Plants, People, and TLC

My houseplants were drooping and some had died. I asked a friend with a green thumb what to do.

"Are you giving your plants lots of TLC?"

I looked at her dubiously. "You don't mean I should . . . er . . . pray for my plants?"

"I suppose that's a good idea." She smiled. "But I was thinking of the actual care. For instance, do you water them properly?"

"Oh, I water regularly once a week."

"Some plants don't need weekly watering, while others need it more often. The plants should be fed as well."

"I didn't know . . ."

"Plant food contains extra nutrients often missing in the soil. And how about repotting?" I looked at her blankly.

"Plants are like people. They often get root-bound and need new depth in which to grow. Or new soil."

"Like a change of environment?"

"Exactly. In fact, some plants thrive best in direct sunlight and others need a shaded spot."

I learned a lot about plants that day and about people. Folks need a healthy environment and proper nourishment. They need prayer too. When cared for properly, they can reach their potential and bloom into the men and women God wants them to be.

❧ TODAY'S DELIGHT:
Water your houseplants. As you do, dust off the leaves,
check the soil, and repot any that are too crowded. As
you do, pray for drought-stricken areas of the world.

Spectrum

*I have set my rainbow in the clouds, and it will be
the sign of the covenant between me and the earth.*

(Genesis 9:13 NIV)

I was on my way to teach a night class in Oregon,
   twelve miles from home.
Black clouds hung over the highway, the aftermath of
   an earlier rainstorm.
Suddenly, the sun burst through a tiny opening in the
   clouds.
As I glanced toward the mountains, I saw a vivid
   rainbow,
stretching from horizon to horizon.
It was so breathtaking I pulled off the highway and
   grabbed my notebook.
I wrote in order, "Purple, blue, green, yellow, orange,
   red."
I'm not sure how long I sat there until the brilliant
   hues dissipated.
Then I became aware I'd been holding my breath,
my pulse had risen,
my entire body was "on alert."
I relaxed long enough to utter a brief prayer of
   thanksgiving
and started the car.
I was only five minutes late for class,
but what a five minutes!

Lord, you promised to see each rainbow in the
   heavens
and remember your everlasting covenant
   with all living creatures. (See Genesis 9:16.)
Thank you for that promise.

❦ *TODAY'S DELIGHT:*
Take special note of the colors in God's creation—a
flower, bush, or a child of God. (If you're lucky, you may
even see a rainbow!)

Only God Can Make a Tree

People can obtain a guidebook to visit our city's oldest residents. Strange, you say? Not when you discover those residents have familiar names such as pine, sycamore, and catalpa. In fact, the catalpa, which measures twenty-one feet seven inches in circumference and has a seventy-nine-foot spread, is the biggest of its kind recorded in the United States.

Forty-one trees—most of them planted around the turn of the century—have been recognized by the Washington State Big Tree Program, an affiliate of the National Big Tree Program sponsored by the American Forestry Association.

Our maple tree hasn't been officially recognized, nor is it included in the walking tour; however, it's a winner in my eyes. Years ago, I wrote a poem trying to express my sentiments.

I do not know what our yard would be
Without that stately maple tree.

True, it's hard for grass to grow
From roots that pop up from below.

We cringe at each box elder bug
That breeds beneath its bark, so snug.

One day my husband said to me,
"Let's cut down that blasted tree!"

But I begged for one more season.
To cut the tree seemed much like treason!

Then, like a prisoner on death row,
Our tree outdid itself to show

That sentencing should be repealed.
And to my mind, new joys revealed.

Its shade seemed cooler than before,
More birds appeared—some by the score.

The leaves were brilliant in the fall.
Of course, we had to rake them all.

But piled-up leaves provided sport
For kids to jump in, and cavort.

Our tree became a revelation
Of a law in God's creation—

That any life is best worth living,
When, for others, it is giving.

Not the best of poetry, but it comes from a thankful heart. It's true, the grass still doesn't grow under the tree. The box elder bugs still thrive. The leaves still need raking (but no longer scattered from jumping kids). As in the story of *The Giving Tree* by Silverstein, our maple tree offers itself with countless more benefits than burdens.

I'm reminded of the last verse in Joyce Kilmer's poem "Trees," which is appropriate here.

Only God Can Make a Tree

> *Poems are made by fools like me,*
> *But only God can make a tree.*

Thank you, God, for trees!

🕊 *TODAY'S DELIGHT:*
Find your favorite tree and enjoy it to the fullest—its
fruit, nuts, shade, branches, leaves. Then thank God for
that tree.

Tenacious Tendrils

Thirty-five years ago when we purchased our home, I diligently nursed a tiny ivy plant at the base of our maple tree. It was all of three inches high.

The tree now reaches skyward one hundred fifty-seven feet. Through the years, the ivy entwined itself around the maple until the vine could be seen in the uppermost branches. Then we were told the ivy could eventually kill our tree, so we decided to cut the climbing plant back.

The ivy's tendrils have small adhesive disks at the end, which tenaciously adhere to the tree's bark. Periodically, I pull down the rapid-growing vine (it can grow from six to ten feet in a single season!). For best results, the ivy needs to be cut off at the base of the tree. Its resilience is especially tough on the east side of the maple, where it gets the most sun.

Would my faith be more dynamic if I clung to the Lord as that ivy clings to the maple tree, or if I started each day facing the "Son"? God can get to the roots of my problems as well, and "cut them off" before they get a stranglehold on me.

The dead vines still cling stubbornly to the bark of our tree, but no longer attached to their source of life, they are downright ugly. We've tried to pull them down, yet even in death they hold fast. (We may hire a tree surgeon with a cherry picker—a mobile crane with a vertical boom—to do the job.)

Likewise, when separated from my Source of Life, I become a slave to sin, which leads to spiritual death and very ugly results. (For more on this concept, read Romans 6.)

I've just learned another lesson from the world of nature around me.

ᏒᎯ *Today's Delight:*
Buy a small plant at your local supermarket or florist, an African violet, pothos, philodendron, or even ivy. (Watch that the ivy doesn't take over your house!)

Grasshopper Expeditions

*A*re not five sparrows sold for two pennies? Yet not
one of them is forgotten in God's sight. . . . You are
of more value than many sparrows.   (Luke 12:6-7 NRSV)

During their college years, our two oldest sons
worked at an onion warehouse. It was one of several
abandoned buildings left standing when a World War
II air base closed down. Open fields surrounded the
area.

One morning the boys found an injured female
sparrow hawk that was unable to fly. After capturing
the tiny bird, they weren't sure what to do with her.
They brought her home in a box, and thus began the
"Summer of the Grasshopper Expeditions."

A friend loaned us an owl cage, which became
Sunny Lou's home. ("Sunny Lou" was a brand name
for the sweet onions our sons processed.)

We did some research and discovered that this
smallest of North America's falcons is considered a
"bird of prey"— one that eats field mice, snakes,
smaller birds, as well as insects. We couldn't furnish
Sunny Lou with most of these morsels, but insects?

The two younger children and I, armed with fly
swatters and glass jars (with lids, of course!), became
great grasshopper hunters. You can't imagine the
speed with which Sunny Lou took a grasshopper from

our fingers, turned the creature headfirst, and slick as a whistle, pulled off the wings, eating the remainder. We must have caught hundreds of grasshoppers during those three months.

But summer soon came to an end, and we were faced with a dilemma. We found Sunny Lou liked stew meat and chicken necks. However, she became lethargic and grew weaker. Our veterinarian sadly informed us that she needed more roughage in her diet, which we could not provide. (And Sunny Lou's injuries were such, she could not have survived in her natural habitat.)

As much as we missed the little bird after her demise, I now look back on that summer and realize my children learned a valuable lesson in caring for a helpless creature. Each day they put the grasshopper expedition before their own play schedules.

God does not forget a sparrow (even a sparrow hawk), and he certainly won't forget us in our daily needs. We may require a helping hand from an outside source, but God can provide that too.

PRAYER:
Father, thank you for your creatures, great and small, and the way in which you provide for their every need.

🍂 TODAY'S DELIGHT:
Do something special for your pet today. Take the dog for a walk, play with your cat (a string on a stick or a

paper bag provide delightful moments). If you have no pet, perhaps you'd like to volunteer to help at your local pet shelter—or give them a donation toward the care of abandoned animals.

Let All Creation Praise

*Let the sea resound, and all that is in it; let the
fields be jubilant, and everything in them. Then all
the trees of the forest will sing for joy; they will sing
before the LORD.* (Psalm 96:11-13 NIV)

There's a line in the wonderful old hymn "This Is My
Father's World" that says, "all nature sings." The
hymn mentions rocks, trees, skies, seas, birds, flowers, and morning light declaring their Maker's praise.

How much singing and praising must old Mother
Nature be doing today? Rarely a day goes by that we
don't read in the newspaper, or see on television, how
we "caretakers" have abused our natural resources.
Truly, the whole creation must be groaning, "as in the
pains of childbirth" (Romans 8:22 NIV).

Throughout the Bible, Scripture personifies nature
as praising its Maker. I think of the following verses:

> The mountains and hills will burst into song
> before you, and all the trees of the field will clap
> their hands. (Isaiah 55:12 NIV)

> Then the trees of the forest will sing, they will
> sing for joy before the LORD, for he comes to
> judge the earth. (1 Chronicles 16:33 NIV)

> The grasslands of the desert overflow; the hills
> are clothed with gladness. The meadows are

covered with flocks and the valleys are mantled
with grain; they shout for joy and sing.

(Psalm 65:12-13 NIV)

We have polluted the seas and other bodies of
water; we have ravaged the earth as we've dug for its
underground treasures; we have overharvested its forests and fields; we have destroyed wildlife until the
government has a list of "endangered species." We
have ignored the pleas of scientists as, in the name of
progress, we have polluted the very air we breathe.

Read aloud "Can I Be Silent?" by Charles H. Spurgeon, quoted at the beginning of this chapter. Ponder
the words and ask the same questions posed by this
celebrated English preacher over one hundred years
ago.

If we joined nature in praising God, would we stand
by and allow his creation to be slowly but steadily
ravaged?

PRAYER:
Lord, when I am careless with your natural resources,
I destroy your handiwork. Make me aware that even
one person can make a difference.

ᐳ *TODAY'S DELIGHT:*
Does your community have a recycling program? If not,
ask your city or town government to provide a "recycling
center" for aluminum and tin cans, cardboard, plastic,

glass, and paper. Think of other ways in which you and your family can help protect the environment.

The privilege of prayer to me is one of the most cherished possessions, because faith and experience alike convince me that God himself sees and answers, and his answers I never venture to criticize. It is only my part to ask. If it were otherwise, I would not dare to pray at all.

—Wilfred T.
Grenfell
(1865–1940)

Delight in Prayer

Prayer is the soul's sincere desire,
Uttered or unexpressed;
The motion of a hidden fire,
That trembles in the breast.

Prayer is the burden of a sigh,
The falling of a tear;
The upward glancing of an eye,
When none but God is near.

—James Montgomery
(1771–1854)

Kneeling Knees—Kneeling Heart

"Where do I start, God?"

I was ready to begin this chapter on "Delight in Prayer," but my ideas were hazy.

"Start on your knees!" The impression was so strong that I immediately knelt by the old green "prayer" rocker in my office.

I was never taught to kneel in prayer as a youngster. I remember with amusement one of my college roommates who faced the problem of kneeling for bedtime prayer. She slept in an upper bunk! However, she never failed to kneel at the lower bunk, choosing a time when its occupant (me) hadn't retired yet. Sometimes she went into the dormitory, prayed, then returned to her room to study.

The Bible is full of illustrations of kneeling pray-ers. A king set an example for his total population in 1 Kings 8:54 and 2 Chronicles 20:18; a whole people knelt in 1 Chronicles 29:29 and Nehemiah 8:6. The disciple Peter knelt to pray (Acts 9:40). The apostle Paul knelt privately (Ephesians 3:14) and with his converts (Acts 20:36). Christ fell on his face and prayed in the Garden of Gethsemane (Matthew 26:39).

I don't think our position matters that much to God; there are examples in the Bible of prayers uttered by people sitting, standing, and even lying down. But I discovered a great difference when I began to pray on my knees.

It's more difficult to fall asleep. My mind doesn't wander as easily. I find it easier to concentrate on the Savior and the character of God. Communication with the Holy Spirit is not strained.

The day may come when I am no longer able to kneel. But I will continue to have a "kneeling" heart as I submit my will to my heavenly Father.

🍂 *TODAY'S DELIGHT:*
Enjoy fellowship with the Father on your knees sometime today. If you cannot kneel physically, do so mentally.

Sitting before the Lord

Then King David went in and sat before the LORD.

(2 Samuel 7:18 NIV)

Several years ago, it was my privilege to hear an inspirational talk by Dr. Charles Stanley. I was so impressed with it, I wrote and asked permission to use points from his message in my speaking ministry.

Ten years have passed since I received permission from Dr. Stanley, and my notes have remained duly filed under "Writers' Conferences." I trust he wouldn't mind my sharing them with you now.

Dr. Stanley took us through David's prayer in 2 Samuel 7:18-29 and highlighted three things.

(1) David *reviewed* his past (verses 18-20). How far has God brought you? What has he saved you from? What have you done with your life?

(2) David *reflected* upon God (verse 22). Do you have others gods in your life? Whatever is constantly on your mind—food, money, sex, recreation, TV—becomes a god to you.

(3) David *remembered* God's promises (verse 28). Do you remember the many promises God has given to you?

Dr. Stanley then asked, "What does it require to sit before the Lord?"

We must learn to be *still.* "Be still, and know that I am God" (Psalm 46:10 NIV).

We must learn to be *silent.* One of my favorite verses comes to mind: "In quietness and in confidence shall be your strength" (Isaiah 30:15).

Jesus often sat before God in *seclusion.* "Very early in the morning . . . Jesus got up . . . and went off to a solitary place, where he prayed" (Mark 1:35 NIV).

Your "solitary" place may be a corner of your living room or kitchen, especially in those morning hours before other family members are awake. God can often do something then that he may do no other time. We must be *sensitive* to God's presence, and start to see things from his perspective. As we become more interested in God doing something *in* us, rather than *for* us, we will develop a *submissive spirit.*

Dr. Stanley suggested several rewards for the person who "sits before the Lord." Our *perspective* definitely changes. What seem like insurmountable problems melt away when seen against the background of God's sovereignty. *Pressures* dissipate. We glibly quote Isaiah 40:31, knowing that if we wait on the Lord, he will renew our strength, but we're not willing to wait for his perfect timing. *Personal* relationships improve, as we begin to achieve inner *purity.* As God unveils the real me, he helps me to become the person he wants me to be. A supernatural *power* is available for all believers, but we often fail to utilize it because we haven't spent quality time with him.

Our effectiveness in serving others is in direct proportion to the time we spend sitting before the Lord.

PRAYER:
Lord, give me a teachable spirit as I humbly sit at your feet. Show me how I may serve others.

❧ *TODAY'S DELIGHT:*
Compare David's prayer in 2 Samuel 7:18-29 and 1 Chronicles 17:16-27. What are the differences, and how do you account for them? (An interesting fact: this prayer is the only reference in the Old Testament to sitting as a posture for prayer.)

The Lord's Prayer

Much has been written about the prayer our Lord taught his disciples. Entire books have dealt with these words of Christ, often called the "perfect" prayer.

The other day I wondered—do I just *say* this prayer, or do I *pray* this prayer? What do the words *really* mean to me? I've tried to express that in poetry.

Our Father
> *Lord, you're Father of every race,*

which art in heaven,
> *You exist beyond time and space.*

Hallowed be thy name.
> *Lord, we always praise your name,*

Thy kingdom come.
> *And believe that earth will be the same*

Thy will be done
> *As heaven is; so earth someday.*

in earth, as it is in heaven.
> *Thy will be done in every way.*

Give us this day
> *Lord, you want us to have bread,*

our daily bread.
> *Your prayer says, daily we'll be fed.*

And forgive us our debts,
You tell us you'll forgive each debt,

as we forgive our debtors.
When we forgive each one we've met.

And lead us not into temptation,
You give us strength for each temptation,

but deliver us from evil:
And guard from wrong in each situation.

For thine is the kingdom, and
Thine the kingdom, power, glory, we pray,

the power, and the glory, for ever.
Forever—as your prayer we say.

Amen.
Amen.

⁖ *TODAY'S DELIGHT:*
Find a book or other resource material on The Lord's Prayer. Concentrate this day on that wonderful prayer. (The above version is found in Matthew 6:9-13 in the King James Version.)

Nudge in the Night

I was awakened abruptly by the awful dream. It was so frightening I was shaking. Why this nightmare about Cathy's marriage? A couple of years before—yes—but not now!

When Cathy was in her twenties, with an infant daughter, her first husband became the victim of a hunting accident. Then she remarried, and two more children joined the family. As she drew closer to God, serving him faithfully, her husband drifted farther away. Then one day, without warning, he took his own life.

Friends prayed Cathy would find a good father for her children, a man with whom she could share her love for God. Tim was that answer, and they had been happily married for several months. So why the bad dream?

Suddenly I had the strong impression to pray for Cathy. I prayed for well over an hour until I finally fell asleep.

The next morning the troubled feeling persisted. I went to the phone, then remembered that Cathy, Tim, and the children were attending a family camp. I continued my intercession and about noon I felt a peace.

Then I had the urge to write Cathy. The following week, I received a reply.

Dear Shirley,

Your letter was awaiting me when we returned from camp. It was a wonderful week, except for one night, when I woke up in great torment about my marriage. I cried bitterly and fought the temptation to walk straight into the lake. All morning I was upset, but around noon, Tim and I sought counseling from one of the leaders. Everything is fine now.

By the way, were you praying for me the night of July 23?

Indeed I was! I am convinced that God woke me up to intercede for my friend. I now try to be obedient to his nudges—night or day!

&❧ *TODAY'S DELIGHT:*
Ask the Lord to bring someone to mind today for whom you can intercede. Then call or write that person a short note.

First appeared in *Standard,* September 7, 1986.

Flash Prayers

The king said to me, "What is it you want?" Then I prayed to the God of heaven, and I answered the king . . . (Nehemiah 2:4-5 NIV)

Nehemiah, a captive Jew in Persia, learned that the city walls around Jerusalem in his homeland were in shambles. God placed within him the desire to have the walls rebuilt. But, as a trusted servant, he first had to get permission from King Artaxerxes to leave.

When an opportunity came, Nehemiah sent a "flash" prayer to God for the proper words to use, and the king was receptive to his request.

Frank Laubach, a great twentieth-century mystic, wrote a book titled, *Prayer—The Mightiest Force in the World,* in which he talks about "flash" prayers. He says, "Everybody in every ordinary day has hundreds of chinks of idle wasted time which may be filled with 'flash prayers' ten seconds or a minute long." He gives the following illustrations:

Upon awakening in the morning
In the bath
Dressing
Walking downstairs
Asking the blessing at table
Leaving the house
Riding or walking to work

Entering the elevator
Preparing for lunch
And a hundred more chinks all day long until
crawling into bed and . . . falling asleep[1]

I can think of dozens more, and so can you.

During television commercials
Waiting for the coffee water to heat in the
microwave
During the prelude and postlude at church
While "on hold" during a business phone call
While timing your three-minute egg

One caution: Don't let these "arrow" prayers become a substitute for spending longer periods of time with the Lord.

Billy Graham put it aptly when he said, "We pray so haphazardly. Snatches of memorized verses are hastily spoken in the morning. Then we say good-bye to God for the rest of the day, until we sleepily push through a few closing petitions at night, like leaving a wake-up call at the hotel switchboard. That is not the example of prayer that Jesus gave. He prayed long and repeatedly.[2]

Paul tells us that we should "pray at all times. . . .

[1] Frank Laubach, *Prayer—The Mightiest Force in the World* (Old Tappan, N.J.: Fleming H. Revell Co., 1946), 73.

[2] Billy Graham, *Hope for the Troubled Heart* (Minneapolis, Minn.: Grason, 1991), 149

This is what God wants of you, in your life in Christ Jesus" (1 Thessalonians 5:17-18 TEV). Graham suggests that this Scripture should be the motto of every true follower of Jesus. "No matter how dark and hopeless a situation might seem, never stop praying. . . . Prayer should be not merely an act, but an attitude of life."[3]

PRAYER:
Lord, teach me to offer spontaneous "flash" prayers, while not neglecting longer times of sweet communion with you.

🙰 *TODAY'S DELIGHT:*
Make your own list of times in your daily schedule when you can send "flash" prayers to God.

[3]Ibid.

On-the-Spot Prayer

I've discovered an exciting new way to pray—on the spot. This may take place in the frozen food aisle of the supermarket or a neighbor's backyard, the church hallway or an airport waiting room. The secret is to pray with a hurting or troubled person right at their moment of need.

I recently conducted a conference with a writing student who confessed she'd fallen behind in her assignments because of difficulty at home. She broke down as she told me she and her husband were considering divorce. I was momentarily at a loss for words. Then I asked gently, "May I pray for you—right now?"

Her eyes widened. Then she whispered, "Would you?" In the quietness of the college classroom, I silently asked the Holy Spirit for guidance, took her hand, and prayed. The following week the couple were trying to work out their differences.

On-the-spot prayer—with the person's permission, of course—spirals a request heavenward immediately and often lifts a heavy burden just as quickly. I know. Someone once prayed for me in women's ready-to-wear. I left the department store with a lighter step and the conviction that I, too, would try to help others through on-the-spot prayers.

On-the-Spot Prayer

This meditation first appeared in *Evangel,* April 12, 1987.

In the Tunnel

I had set aside two entire days for writing. How I looked forward to it! Then I was stricken with a nasty bout of stomach flu. The second day I was so weak and sore, writing again had to be postponed. So much for my good intentions!

Have you ever noticed how introverted we become when we are ill? Our mind can't operate beyond the physical limitations our body places upon us. We're in a tunnel where *self* rules supreme, blocking any light that might shine through.

Some years ago at a writers' conference, author Philip Yancey spoke about "backward tunnel vision." He suggested that too often writing is done from a viewpoint *after* we've been through the tunnel, and in so doing, we are unable to best describe the ordeal of suffering.

That's why I was so impressed when I read the following in Anne Ortlund's *The Disciplines of the Beautiful Woman:*[1]

> This is November 20, 1975; two days past November 18, which was hysterectomy day for me. [Two days after major surgery?]
> Now at last my eyes are just beginning to focus; the mountains are beautiful out my

[1] Anne Ortlund, *The Disciplines of the Beautiful Woman* (Waco, Tex.: Word Books, 1977), 10-12.

window; my bed is rolled up into a sitting position, and I can once more put words on paper. A
little. I'll pick at it. [Using her God-given gift of
writing despite the pain!]

She goes on to finish that chapter:

I'm living a very full life right here in bed, two
days after surgery. I'm practicing the presence of
God; I'm enjoying thoughts of him and all his
goodness; and when I'm "up again, out again," I
trust my life will be just as full as it is right
now—full of him.

Mrs. Ortlund suggests that "pain is God's beautiful
gift . . . to make us lean harder on him, when he
knows we need it. Or pain can simply be the means to
that quiet we so long for."

C. S. Lewis called pain "the megaphone of God." Dr.
Paul Brand, the famous leprosy doctor, says sincerely,
"Thank God for pain!"[2]

Pain, more than many other factors in our life, can
turn us to prayer. It certainly did the dynamic Christians mentioned above, and prayer can turn my "self"
thoughts to the Creator of this intricate body of mine.

[2] Philip Yancey, *Where Is God When It Hurts?* (Grand Rapids,
Mich.: Zondervan, 1977), 29, 55.

🍂 *TODAY'S DELIGHT:*
Send a card to a person in pain. (It may be someone
suffering from emotional rather than physical pain.)
Assure him or her of your love and prayers, but don't
preach! You might want to pass along some reading
material, such as Philip Yancey's Where Is God When
It Hurts?

That's Mighty Fast!

I will answer them before they even call to me.
While they are still talking to me about their needs,
I will go ahead and answer their prayers!

(Isaiah 65:24 TLB)

I was lamenting the fact that it had taken a letter from Michigan eight days to reach me, when I read the following in the local paper:

"It appears that a helium balloon released in Walla Walla Wednesday was found in New York one day later. By air, that's about two thousand one hundred miles in around twenty-four hours."

The article went on to say that the balloon was one of one hundred released by the local Oddfellows Home as part of National Nursing Home Week. Each balloon contained a note, "Have a good day, from the Washington Oddfellows." A few days later, the home received a letter from a lady in Natural Bridge, New York, saying the balloon had been found by her eight-year-old son and a neighbor boy.

According to the National Weather Service, such occurrences are unlikely but possible, since winds at the upper levels travel up to one hundred and twenty miles per hour.

That balloon traveled mighty fast! What's even more surprising is God's supernatural delivery service. We send a prayer winging its way into the heavenlies, and before we've even finished speaking the words, God is answering. We may not be aware of the results that quickly, but God has done his part. We must trust him for the outcome.

In case you've lost God's phone number, it's easy to remember—just three threes, Jeremiah 33:3: "Call to me and I will answer you and tell you great and unsearchable things you do not know" (NIV).

By the way, my brother had inadvertently omitted the zip code on that letter from Michigan. Even so, it took a postcard mailed at the same time four days!

PRAYER:
After I pray to you, Lord, quiet me down so that I may hear your answer. If I don't hear you immediately, please give me patience to wait.

❧ *TODAY'S DELIGHT:*
Buy a packet of balloons and with a contrasting marker, write messages on them. When the occasion arises, blow one up and give it to someone needing one of the messages, such as "Thinking of You!" "You're Great!" "Have a Good Day!" "In My Prayers!" "Get Well Soon!"

Unseen Battles

A young friend is on the mission field with her husband in a South American country. Due to terrorist activity, there have been serious threats to the mission station. Those supporting the couple pray for them continually.

In a recent letter, Pam shared a story that filtered back to them from an enemy stronghold.

One night terrorists *did* come. They found the area surrounded by "armed men" and were unable to inflict any damage. The folks at the mission were asleep and heard nothing.

"Who were our guards that night?" Pam asks. She adds, "It's been some time since we've received any threats, although terrorist activity continues in other places. How can we thank you enough for your prayer support?"

We read of a similar account in 2 Kings 6, in which the king of Syria and his forces surrounded the city of Dothan. Elisha's servant was terror-stricken until the man of God prayed, "O Lord, open his eyes." Can you imagine the servant's amazement to see the surrounding hills full of horses and chariots of fire? Then Elisha prayed that the enemy army be struck with blindness.

I've read similar documented examples of God's intervention through angel warriors from World Wars I and II. They have included phantom horsemen, camels, even bombers. There are those who feel that angels played an important role in the Persian Gulf War as well.

We must never underestimate the power of intercession for "the prayer of the righteous is powerful and effective" (James 5:16 NRSV).

> *TODAY'S DELIGHT:*
> *Write to a missionary serving your church on foreign soil. Pray for him or her daily.*

Jelly Bean Prayer

My husband is an avid fisherman. So when he came down with a bad cold, his fishing buddy brought over a special remedy.

It was a jar labeled "Fishing Control Pills" from the *Can-of-Worms Pharmacy*. The "pills" had been prescribed by Dr. Rod N. Reel and were surprisingly shaped like jelly beans. In fact, they *were* jelly beans!

They reminded me of a prayer a friend once sent me. Since the author is unknown, I am free to share it with you.

> *The Jelly Bean Prayer*
>
> *Red is for the blood he gave,*
> *Green is for the grass he made.*
> *Yellow is for his sun so bright,*
> *Orange is for the edge of night.*
> *Black is for the sins we made,*
> *White is for the grace he gave.*
> *Purple is for his hours of sorrow,*
> *Pink is for our new tomorrow.*
> *A bagful of jelly beans—colorful and sweet,*
> *Is a prayer, a promise, and a small child's treat.*

When I caught Kyle's cold, I found the prescription to be amazingly effective! Of course, I took them with cold tablets and with high dosages of prayer, including the one on the previous page. It changed my perspective on jelly beans!

ða *TODAY'S DELIGHT:*
Buy a bag of jelly beans. As you eat them, let each color remind you of the above objects in the poem.

Alongside a Barley Field

Throughout the years, I've belonged to several prayer groups that met at a variety of times. I especially remember one from my young motherhood days that met in the home of a woman with older children. But when summer came, we were stumped. Lettice planned to attend summer school, and the rest of us had youngsters whose vacation schedules made a home prayer meeting difficult.

After two weeks of inactivity, we realized how much we missed the prayer group.

"Why not meet in our cars?" Barbara suggested. At first we scoffed, then decided to try it.

I'll never forget that first mobile prayer meeting.

We drove toward the foothills and parked alongside a barley field. The amber heads of grain swayed in the breeze. A favorite psalm came alive as we viewed awe-inspiring mountains in the distance: "I look to the mountains; where will my help come from? My help will come from the Lord, who made heaven and earth" (Psalm 121:1-2, TEV).

For the next three months we joined the author of Psalm 148 (TEV) as he praised the Creator:

"Praise the Lord! Praise the Lord from heaven. . . . Praise him, sun and moon [we had prayed beneath a full moon]. . . . Praise him, shining stars [we'd watched the stars, one by one, pop out and twinkle at us]. . . . Praise the Lord from the earth [we were earthbound and yet!] . . . strong winds that obey his command [we watched the approach of a thunderstorm] . . . all animals, tame and wild, reptiles and birds [we had seen a coyote running across a distant field and heard the night call of the meadowlark] . . . girls and young men, old people and children too" [(we laughed uproariously as a group of teenage boys sped past, slammed on their brakes, then discovered we were only a carload of women almost old enough to be their mothers!)].

When fall arrived, we returned to Lettice's home. But we would never again close our minds to innovative ways to pray and to worship God—even in a car, alongside a barley field!

❧ *TODAY'S DELIGHT:*
Drive to a rural setting, if possible, or walk to a nearby park. Spend time there in prayer, praising God for his amazing creation.

This devotion is partially adapted from an article by the same title, which first appeared in *Power for Living,* April 10, 1981.

In Any Language

For God so loved the world, that he gave his only begotten Son, that whosoever believeth in him should not perish, but have everlasting life.

(John 3:16)

We once knew a young Norwegian man who worked on a cruise ship. His working schedule brought long separations from his wife and little girl. But he tried to learn to rely upon the Lord during those difficult times.

While visiting relatives in Norway, this young man had a special touch from God. He wrote to me and asked, "Do you think God understands Norwegian prayers?" He received my answer after he returned to the States. As he read my letter, he suddenly called out to his wife, "Did you know Shirley knows Norwegian?"

Actually, I don't. But while on a trip, I'd picked up a Gideon Bible in a hotel room and discovered a familiar Bible passage in several languages. I copied the Norwegian words.

For sa har Gud elsket verden at han gav sin sonn, den enbarne, forat hver den som tror pa ham, ikke skal fortapes, men ha evig liv.

God speaks John 3:16 in over three thousand spoken languages, plus all of the dialects in the world. He understands and listens to devout prayers uttered in them all.

PRAYER:
Thank you, Lord, that you hear our prayers in any language, as well as our unspoken prayers. Thank you for sending your Son for all people.

ᘒ *TODAY'S DELIGHT:*
If possible, learn John 3:16 in another language. Or share it in English with someone who needs to know this great truth.

There is always sunshine somewhere for which I praise God—the sunshine that brightens other lives when mine is shrouded in gloom. Glory to Thee, my God, for the gladness of little children, for the joy of mothers, for the bliss of lovers. The radiance of their hearts is from Thy touch because in the joy of Thy creation Thou rejoicest. And I praise Thee, my God, that in my unhappiest days there are breaks in the clouds through which I see the blue beyond and the glorious sun of Thy compassionate love. Even a moment of light gives me new hope and new courage.

—Charles H. Brent
(1862–1929)

Delight in Worship and Praise

Whatever the thing may be—
if it humbles us,
if it gives us a vision of duty,
if it exalts us,
if it sends us back into the busy world
with a steadying hand upon us,
and if, above all, it makes us aware
of God—
it is worship.

—_Boynton Merrill,_ Words of Life

Three Honest Serving Men
(What, Why, and When)

Rudyard Kipling probably didn't know he'd come up with the ideal formula for journalists when he wrote in his classic *The Elephant's Child* the following words:

> *I keep six honest serving men*
> *(They taught me all I knew);*
> *Their names are What and Why and When*
> *And How and Where and Who.*

A few years ago I applied the "Five *W*s Plus *H*" to a study on the worship of God. It helped me get a grasp on the vastness of our relationship to God through worship and praise. If you enjoy the challenge of searching the Scriptures, take time in the next few days to look up the references found in this and the next selection.

Following Kipling's pattern, we start with WHAT.

Simply stated, the WHAT of our worship is God himself. The Athenians had erected an altar to an unknown god, lest they forget one of the many deities worshiped in their city. Paul told them, "Now WHAT you worship as something unknown I am going to proclaim to you" (Acts 17:23 NIV [emphasis mine]).

WHY do we worship God? We must look at this question from two points of view—that of God and that of humans.

From God's point of view:
- God is worthy of worship and praise—Psalm 18:3.
- God commands it—Psalm 96:7-9
- Worship is a way of entering into his presence—Psalm 100:4.
- Worship is a way of honoring him—Psalm 50:23.
- Worship is a good witness to others—Psalm 40:3.

From the human point of view:
- Worship helps us become God-centered—James 4:8.
- Worship keeps our mind on him—Isaiah 26:3.
- Worship releases God's power and presence—Acts 16:25-26.
- Worship gives us thankful hearts—Colossians 3:15.
- Worship changes us into God's image—2 Corinthians 3:18.

WHEN do we worship God?
- We worship him daily—Psalm 145:2.
- We worship him morning, noon, and evening—Psalm 55:17.
- We can even worship him at midnight—Psalm 119:62.
- We worship him as long as we live—Psalm 104:33.
- In fact, our worship continues forever and ever—Psalm 45:17.

The next meditation will deal with the remaining "honest serving men"—HOW, WHERE, and WHO.

&❧ *TODAY'S DELIGHT:*
Look up praise *and* worship *in a concordance. Then set aside part of your quiet time during the next few days to check the references. Your attitude of praise and worship will grow by leaps and bounds.*

Three More Serving Men
(How, Where, and Who)

The Bible suggests many ways of HOW to worship God. We should especially be aware of John's admonition: "They that worship him must worship him in spirit and in truth" (John 4:24).

With that fact established, let's move on to HOW to worship God with our voices, hands, and bodies.

VOICE:
1. Mouth (speaking)—Psalm 51:15; 71:15; 145:21.
2. Singing—2 Chronicles 20:21-22; Psalm 98:1; 104:33.
3. Shouting—Psalm 32:11 (KJV); 47:1; Isaiah 12:6.

HANDS:
1. Clapping—Psalm 47:1.
2. Lifting up—Psalm 63:4; 134:2; 1 Timothy 2:8.
3. Playing instruments—1 Chronicles 25:6; Psalm 33:2-3; 150:3-5.

BODY:
1. Standing—1 Chronicles 23:30; Nehemiah 9:5; Mark 11:25.
2. Bowing or kneeling—Psalm 95:6; Daniel 6:10; Philippians 2:10.
3. Dancing—Exodus 15:20 (Miriam); 2 Samuel 6:14 (David); Psalm 149:3.

WHERE do we worship God? Numerous references suggest that we worship wherever we find ourselves in our daily walk. Examples of corporate expressions of worship are found in 2 Chronicles 29:28-32, Psalm 35:18, and Hebrews 10:25.

WHO is to worship God?

- All servants of the Lord should praise him—Psalm 113:1; Revelation 19:5.
- All nations and peoples—Psalm 117:1.
- Heaven and earth join together to praise and worship—Psalm 69:34.
- Everything that has breath should praise the Lord—Psalm 150:6.

If you're a bit confused in differentiating between *worship* and *praise,* this definition has helped me: Worship is "bowing down" to God, and praise is "lifting up" to God. Praise is the anteroom in which we spend time before entering the great cathedral of worship.

Praise and worship are so intertwined that they are used interchangeably in different versions of the Bible.

❧ *TODAY'S DELIGHT:*
As time allows, look up the above verses and those in the preceding meditation. Then spend some time in worship and praise in whatever way is comfortable for you.

Is There a Worthiness to Our Worship?

At this writing, I'm eagerly looking forward to a trip to the Holy Land. We will first stay in Tiberias on the Sea of Galilee and visit such surrounding sites as Capernaum, Cana, Nazareth, and Megiddo. After a stop at Haifa and Mount Carmel, we then move on to Jerusalem, with side trips to Bethlehem and Masada.

One of the most fascinating places in Jerusalem will likely be the Dome of the Rock, that historic spot where, for centuries, the Jewish temple stood. Solomon's temple, built around 950 B.C., was destroyed by invading Babylonians in 586 B.C. Fifty years later, returning Jewish exiles built a second temple (very modest in comparison to Solomon's). Centuries later, it was expanded by Herod the Great (20 B.C.–A.D. 64, and it was here that Jesus taught and preached. This temple was completely demolished by the Romans in A.D. 70. Today, the Dome of the Rock is controlled by the Muslims.

Yet that rock, actually the summit of Mount Moriah, goes back in Judeo-Christian history to the time of Abraham's near-sacrifice of his son Isaac. In David's time, it was used as a threshing floor, owned by a man named Araunah (known as Ornan in 1 Chronicles 21). When David wanted to build an altar on it, Araunah told him, "Let my lord the king take whatever pleases him and offer it up. . . . O king, Araunah gives all this to the king" (2 Samuel 24:22-23 NIV).

David's answer is of great significance. "No, I insist on paying you for it. I will not sacrifice to the LORD my God burnt offerings that cost me nothing" (24:24). David then paid for Araunah's threshing floor and the oxen he had offered for sacrifice, and built an altar to the Lord there.

Jack Hayford says, "He [David] knew worship should have a worthiness including an open hand as well as an open heart."[1]

How difficult for those who are tightfisted and hardhearted to worship God. Yet I must ask myself, do I tithe begrudgingly, with fingers that must be pried apart? Or do I offer my gifts to the Father with an open hand? Is my heart open to receive all that God wants to give me?

Is there a worthiness to my worship?

❧ *TODAY'S DELIGHT:*
Draw a picture of an open hand and a heart. (Or, if like me, you can't draw well, cut pictures from a magazine.) Post them in a conspicuous place—the bathroom mirror, the dashboard of your car, above your typewriter or computer, on the refrigerator door. Across the hand and the heart write something like, "Thou art worthy"

[1] Jack Hayford, *Worship His Majesty* (Waco, Tex.: Word Books, 1987), 172.

Is There a Worthiness to Our Worship?

(Revelation 4:11), or "Lead a life worthy of God"
(1 Thessalonians 2:12 NRSV).

Forget the Time!

Have you ever caught yourself glancing at your watch
in church when noontime approaches?
Dad wonders if he's going to miss the kickoff of the
pro game on TV.
Mom reminds herself to turn the oven on when she
gets home.

Last week I visited a Hispanic congregation.
Such mundane things weren't on their minds!
How these folks worship the Lord!
They put me to shame!
I understood very few words, but as I listened to the
joyous singing and the "Hallelujahs" that peppered
the air, I became caught up in their worship.

I recently read of a church in Kenya where members
arrive early in the morning and stay most of the day.
They hear sermons by pastors and laymen, and sing
at the top of their lungs.
When the service draws to a close in the late
afternoon, church members parade in different
directions down dirt roads, singing and beating
drums.
When curious crowds form, a pastor preaches and
challenges listeners to receive Christ.

Forget the Time!

Unlike you and me, these Kenyans don't glance at
    their watches.
They are too poor to own one!

&❧ *TODAY'S DELIGHT:*
*Next Sunday, don't wear a watch to church! Forget the
time and concentrate on worshiping and praising the
Lord. (But check a clock at home, so you're not late for
services!)*

Old Wine—Old Skins

If you were born between 1945 and 1964, your generation has been dubbed the "baby boomers."

One day you decide to visit a new church. An old person greets you at the door and hands you a badly mimeographed bulletin. You sit in a hard pew and stare at the back of someone's head. You hear a twenty-minute talk on theology and sing four-hundred-year-old songs. Just before leaving, they ask you for money. Oh yes, there is a coffee hour after the worship service, but you feel like you've walked into someone else's high school reunion. You decide that church attendance is not for you!

Does that describe my church—or yours? I hope not! There's nothing wrong with older greeters (I'm one myself) or with singing some of the wonderful old hymns of the church.

Jesus warned against trying to put new wine in old wineskins, but the above description sounds more like old wineskins holding old wine.

I want to worship God in new ways without forsaking meaningful traditions that have been handed down from generations of saintly folks.

Do you suppose baby boomers want the same things? If so, how can I help to make my church attractive and reach out to those of a younger generation?

❧ *TODAY'S DELIGHT:*
Invite a younger couple or family into your home. Share
spiritual highlights from your own walk with the Lord.
If the Lord leads, invite them to attend church with you.
However, be aware that your sharing may be in action,
rather than words.

A Sure Defense

I will call upon the Lord, who is worthy to be praised; he will save me from all my enemies.

(2 Samuel 22:4 TLB)

My husband and I rented a car and spent a month traveling throughout England and Scotland. Among all the historical sights, those we found the most fascinating were the medieval castles scattered throughout Great Britain.

A few of my favorites were Bodiam, Warwick, and Leeds castles, the latter two painstakingly restored both inside and out. Leeds is considered by many to be "the loveliest castle in the world." Bodiam, on the other hand, while just a skeleton, has well-preserved outer walls and towers, enabling the visitor to view the simplicity of the original pattern. All three of these castles are mirrored in the moats surrounding them.

These water-filled moats are mute reminders of the efforts of early inhabitants to defend themselves from invasion. Even a cursory study of Great Britain's history attests to the many enemy attacks.

Within the walls of Warwick and Leeds castles, we saw collections of armor and weapons with which medieval soldiers equipped themselves.

From Jesus' time to this day, the Enemy's assaults have tried to destroy Christianity. But Christians have far more effective protection.

We are surrounded by a moat of Living Water—
Christ, our Lord (see John 4:10). We wear God's
armor, consisting of a belt of truth, a breastplate of
righteousness, shoes of peace, a shield of faith, a
helmet of salvation, and a sword of the Spirit which is
the Word of God (Ephesians 6:13-17).

As you remain steadfast in your faith and resist
Satan, God "personally will come and pick you up, and
set you firmly in place, and make you stronger than
ever" (1 Peter 5:10 TLB).

PRAYER:
God, thank you for being my sure defense. Help me to
stand firm in all the trials that come my way.

❧ *TODAY'S DELIGHT:*
*As a child, you played the game of "Let's Pretend." So
now I challenge you to try this experiment. As you dress
each morning, envision yourself putting on God's armor.
Fasten the belt of truth as you put on your slacks or
skirt; put into place the breastplate of righteousness as
you don your shirt or blouse. When you slip into your
shoes, picture them as shoes of peace; when combing
your hair, place upon your head the helmet of salvation.
Begin your morning worship by visualizing the shield of
faith protecting your mind from interruptions. Then
pick up the sword of the Spirit, God's Word, and know
that you are surrounded by the "moat" of Living Water.
I think you'll like your new outfit!*

Do You Believe in Signs?

Blessed are those who have not seen and yet believe.

(John 20:29 RSV)

On a stretch of Interstate 84 through Idaho, the route climbs to Sweetzer Summit. I saw signs such as Deer Migration Area and Deer Crossing, as well as a picture of a leaping deer.

Alerted, I began to drive more defensively, but I didn't see a single four-legged creature. Hmm! Were the signs untrue? Of course not! I had enough faith in the Idaho State Highway Department to believe their signs even if no animals were spotted.

As I drove along, my mind was drawn to the similarities with the Holy Spirit. I cannot see, touch, or hear the Spirit, but there are signposts all around me that point to his existence.

I *hear* the Holy Spirit speaking through great men and women of God, from the pulpit, sometimes via radio or television.

I *see* words about the Holy Spirit in the Bible. I *see* him at work in the lives of his everyday saints.

I *feel* the Holy Spirit through the loving touch of his followers and through his presence in my own life.

Just as I became alert to the deer signs on I-84, I want to become aware of the "dear" signs on my highway of life—the dear fellowship of the Holy Spirit.

Do You Believe in Signs?

Quicken my senses to your leading, Holy Spirit. Help
me to *see, hear,* and *feel* your presence this day as I
praise the Lord.

❧ *TODAY'S DELIGHT:*
Buy a "sign" for your home—perhaps a picture of
Christ, or the Christian fish symbol for your front door.

God's Morning Love

He wakens me morning by morning, wakens my ear to listen like one being taught. (Isaiah 50:4 NIV)

Donna and I realized we weren't starting our days often enough with the Lord. So we made a covenant to call each other every morning at 6:45 to spend fifteen minutes worshiping and praising God. We wanted to tell him how much we appreciated him and ask for guidance throughout the day.

The first morning we asked the Lord to show us how he wanted us to pray. A pattern emerged whereby we took turns sharing Scriptures, prayers written by others, our own personal prayers, and often words from a hymn.

We became increasingly aware that the majority of hymns are based on a line or two of Scripture. They fit perfectly into our new prayer time. The other morning I ran across the hymn, "Speak, Lord, in the Stillness." It is based on 1 Samuel 3:10: "The LORD came and stood there, calling. . . . Then Samuel said, 'Speak, for your servant is listening'" (NIV). Too often, my prayers are prefaced with the words, "Listen, Lord, for your servant speaks." Donna and I are trying to listen to the Lord during the quiet morning time.

Our new practice is changing each day's outlook.

Our attitudes, thoughts, and actions are coming in line with his will for our lives.

Why should we be so surprised? He has promised that his mercies and compassions are new and fresh every morning (Lamentations 3:22-23); that joy comes in the morning (Psalm 30:5) as does his unfailing love (Psalm 143:8).

By the way, we have also embarked on a regimen of memorizing Scripture. (See "Other Memory Tricks" on page 202-204.

PRAYER:
Lord, what do you want me to *do* today? What do you want me to *be* today? This morning I will sing of your strength and your love (Psalm 59:16).

❧ *TODAY'S DELIGHT:*
Is there someone with whom you can spend fifteen minutes in the early hours of each day? Perhaps someone else in your household, or someone on the phone? If not possible, God will, of course, speak to you alone in the stillness. Try to establish a special appointment with him—beginning tomorrow morning.

He Makes Everything New

See, I am doing a new thing! (Isaiah 43:19 NIV)

He who was seated on the throne said, "I am making everything new!" (Revelation 21:5 NIV)

It was lunchtime. Yet the cans of soup, the cold cuts, the peanut butter jar did not appeal to me.

"How about a bowl of cold cereal?" I asked myself. Whoever heard of cold cereal for lunch? What an impulsive idea!

On the other hand, why not? Apprehensively, I poured myself a bowl of granola. I felt a little odd as I dug in with my spoon. Then I began laughing and gave myself permission to eat a second bowlful.

Several years ago, while shopping at a local drugstore, I smelled something familiar, a scent that reminded me of my childhood. My nose led me to a display of candles. The label on the box read "Citronella, Insect Repellent." Then I remembered! Mother used to slather us with oil of citronella to keep the pesky mosquitoes from chewing on our arms and legs. Same ingredient, but in a different form.

These two experiences caused me to ask myself—why are so many of us uncomfortable when our church tries different forms of worship?

Wasn't it better to light a candle than to slather

sticky oil on the body? Didn't the cold cereal satisfy
my hunger, even if not "traditional" lunch fare? Don't
innovative ways of worship serve as a vehicle for
praising our Lord?

God has never limited the way he communicates
with us. He tried to get his message across to his
chosen ones through the patriarchs and the prophets.
Then he dared to do something earthshakingly different. He sent his Son to dwell among us. Christ told his
followers that after his death the Father would send a
"Comforter," a "Helper," the Holy Spirit—not just to
live *among* them, but *in* them!

So sit back and relax the next time your church
tries a new form of worship. Let God minister to you
in a *new* way!

PRAYER:
Lord, help me to take a step of faith that dares to be
different—to enjoy the new things you are doing in
my church—and in my life.

ᘍ *TODAY'S DELIGHT:*
Visit a church that worships in a different manner from
your regular congregation. Or try new forms of worship
in the privacy of your home—sing a song of praise to the
Lord, raise your hands while praying, kneel during
prayer, or clap your hands, all of which are scriptural.
(There are even a half-dozen examples in the Bible of
worshipers dancing before the Lord!)

A Praise Diary

*It is a good thing to give thanks unto the LORD,
and to sing praises unto thy name, O Most High.*

(Psalm 92:1)

I've kept a diary for years. I record daily happenings,
errands, chores, meetings—in other words, the
nitty-gritty of everyday life. I also write down my
frustrations, heartaches, and pains. Frankly, my diary
makes dull reading!

What a difference when I began to keep a praise
diary. It's designed for *one* thing—PRAISE!

Recently I thought back to a hurtful experience that
had filled me with self-pity for several days. Then I
wondered, What did I record in my praise diary
during that time?

I could hardly believe my eyes! I'd praised God for
telephones, a Sunday sermon, photocopy machines, a
hair set, my cat's antics, frost on the neighbor's birch
tree. One day I'd simply written, "Praise for being
alive!"

An attitude of praise brings us much closer to God.
In Psalm 22:3, we are told that God inhabits the
praises of his people.

A praise diary will lift your spirits when you "fill
your minds with those things that are good and
deserve praise: things that are true, noble, right, pure,
lovely, and honorable" (Philippians 4:8 TEV).

333

A Praise Diary

PRAYER:
Lord, teach me to praise you every day, regardless of circumstances in my life.

ᶻ❧ *TODAY'S DELIGHT:*
Buy a steno pad or an inexpensive notebook, and start a praise diary.

Sing Praise to God

*Speak to one another in psalms, hymns, and
sacred songs. Sing praise to God with all your
hearts.* (Ephesians 5:19, Goodspeed)

I have developed a strange cough that is aggravated
when I try to sing. Recently I attended a three-day
retreat and was so frustrated whenever the singing
began. I hadn't realized the importance of music in
my praise to God.

Music also plays an important part in the medical
field. One neurologist feels that the power of music
"may move those who can't walk to dance, those who
can't speak to sing, those who can't remember
to—well, remember."[1]

Another says that music therapy helps those with
memory losses, adding that songs often bring back
memories of courtship, a wedding, or some other
highlight of the person's life.

Throughout the Bible, people remembered important events by setting them to music and then praising
God through song. Among those whose songs of
praise have been recorded in Scripture are Moses,
Deborah, Barak, Solomon, Isaiah, Mary (Jesus'

---

[1] Susan L. Crowley, "The Amazing 'Power of Music,'" *AARP
Bulletin,* Washington, D.C.

mother), Zacharias, and, of course, David, whose songs make up almost half of the book of Psalms.

A footnote in my Bible points out that "music and singing were a cherished part of Israel's culture," and that "songs of praise focus our attention on God, give us an outlet for spiritual celebration, and remind us of God's faithfulness and character."[2]

I like the Phillips paraphrase of the above verse: "Sing among yourselves psalms and hymns and spiritual songs, your voices making music in your hearts for the ears of the Lord!"

Although I could not praise God audibly that retreat weekend, I chose to make music in my heart, knowing that it was, after all, for the ears of the Lord, and not for those sitting around me.

PRAYER:
Father, whether aloud or silently within my heart, I praise you with song today.

⋙ TODAY'S DELIGHT:
Many psalms refer to singing as a way of praising God. See how many you can find. Here are a few to get you started:

Come, let us sing for joy to the LORD.

(Psalm 95:1 NIV)

---

[2] Footnotes on Judges 5:1ff., New Revised Standard Version of the *Life Application Bible,* (Wheaton, Ill.: Tyndale House Publishers, 1989), 376.

O sing to the LORD a new song.

(Psalm 98:1 RSV)

I will sing to the Lord as long as I live. I will
praise God to my last breath!

(Psalm 104:33 TLB)

Many Crowns

*His eyes are like blazing fire, and on his head are
many crowns.*   (Revelation 19:12 NIV)

I've always felt an affinity to Queen Elizabeth. She is a
year younger than I am, her birthday three days prior
to mine. She gave birth to three boys and a girl, as did
I. Some say we physically resemble each other. The
similarities stop there.

I am awed when I see pictures of the queen wearing
the Imperial State Crown. On a visit to the Tower of
London, we saw this crown, originally made for
Queen Victoria's coronation in 1838. Once a year, at
the state opening of Parliament, Queen Elizabeth
rides in a royal carriage from Buckingham Palace
and, wearing the Imperial State Crown, delivers a
speech from the throne in the House of Lords.

The crown is the most valuable piece of jewelry in
the world and weighs two-and-a-half pounds. It is
studded with four huge "Star of Africa" diamonds, the
second of which weighs three hundred seventeen
carats and is set in the front of the band just above an
edging of ermine. The most historic jewel in the
crown, the Black Prince's ruby, was worn by Henry V
at the Battle of Agincourt. From the intersection of
two diamond-encrusted arches hang four drop pearls,
reputedly the earrings of Queen Elizabeth I. The

crown is topped by a cross; in the center is St. Edward's sapphire, taken from a ring worn by Edward the Confessor.

Aside from these historical stones, the crown contains five rubies, eleven emeralds, eighteen sapphires, two hundred seventy-seven pearls, and two thousand seven hundred eighty-three diamonds![1]

Doesn't that make your head swirl? As impressed as I am with Britain's Imperial State Crown, I am actually more impressed with heaven's crowns, which *I* will someday wear. The Bible tells of a crown of righteousness (2 Timothy 4:8), an incorruptible crown (1 Corinthians 9:25), a crown of rejoicing (1 Thessalonians 2:19), a crown of steadfast love and mercy (Psalm 103:4), a crown of glory (1 Peter 5:4), a crown of life (James 1:12).

What will I do with my many crowns? Place them on my head? Clutch them to my bosom? No, I will join other saints as I lay my crowns before the throne. I'll raise my voice and sing with the others: "Thou art worthy, O Lord, to receive glory and honour and power: for thou hast created all things, and for thy pleasure they are and were created" (Revelation 4:11).

PRAYER:
Lord, I want to make sure heaven's crowns fit me.

[1] Much of this description was taken from *The Queen and Her Court,* by Jerrold M. Packard (New York: Charles Scribner's Sons, 1981), 156–157.

Help me to live a life of righteousness, joy, love, and mercy. Amen.

ᴥ *TODAY'S DELIGHT:*
Find a hymnal and sing "Crown Him with Many Crowns." The text was written by two nineteenth-century Anglican rectors, Matthew Bridges and Godfrey Thring. In its many verses, we are admonished to "Crown him the Lord of life, of peace, of love, of heaven, of years . . . and to crown him the Son of God."

Delight in Sharing with Youngsters

*A special chapter designed for you to share
with the special youngsters in your life.*

SOMEWHERE THE CHILD

Among the thousands of tiny things
growing up all over the land, some of
them under my very wing—watched
and tended, unwatched and untended,
loved, unloved, protected from danger,
thrust into temptation—among them
somewhere is the child who will write
the novel that will stir men's hearts
to nobler issues and incite them to
better deeds.

There is the child who will paint the
greatest picture or carve the greatest
statue of the age; another who will
deliver his country in an hour of peril;

another who will give his life for a great principle; and another, born more of the spirit than of the flesh, who will live continually on the heights of moral being, and dying, draw men after him.

It may be that I shall preserve one of these children to the race. It is a peg big enough on which to hang a hope, for every child born into the world is a new incarnate thought of God, an ever fresh and radiant possibility.

—*Kate Douglas Wiggin*
(1856–1923)

Be Glad You're You!

I praise you because I am fearfully and wonderfully made. (Psalm 139:14 NIV)

"Why, you look just like your dad!"

"Your hair is the same color as your grandmother's." Has anyone ever said something like that to you? Maybe you don't like to be told you look like your parents or grandparents.

On the other hand, your older sister may be beautiful, and you wish your hair or eyes were just like hers. Or your brother gets all *A*'s, and you wish you were as smart as he.

God didn't make a mistake when he gave you your eyes, nose, mouth, or hair. He didn't make a mistake when he gave you your brain. In fact, Psalm 139 says he knows all your thoughts. He knows when you sit down and stand up. God even knows what you're going to say before you say it!

Yes, God knew ahead of time how you would look, talk, and act. Nobody else in the entire world is exactly like you.

So next time you complain about your looks, your size, or your intelligence, remember: *You are very special to God!*

Be Glad You're You!

Dear God, thank you for making me just the way you
did and for loving me just the way I am.

🔖 *TODAY'S DELIGHT:*
Have somebody take a picture of you—with a big smile
on your face. Write the above Scripture on the back. In
years to come, you will enjoy looking at the picture and
remembering this day.

Morning Time

Very early in the morning . . . Jesus got up . . . and went off to a solitary place, where he prayed.

(Mark 1:35)

Is it difficult to open your eyes in the morning? Are you crabby when you first wake up? Does Mother have to call you several times?

Perhaps you stayed up too long watching television. Or you're worried about a problem at home or school. God gives you more than daylight each morning. Listen to what the Bible has to say (emphasis on verses mine):

REJOICING comes in the morning.   (Psalm 30:5)

Let the morning bring me word of your *UNFAILING LOVE.*   (Psalm 143:8)

Be our *STRENGTH* every morning.   (Isaiah 33:2)

In the morning, O LORD, you *HEAR* my voice.

(Psalm 5:3)

If you want to have God's *JOY, LOVE, STRENGTH,* and know that he *HEARS* you, there are things you must do:

In the morning *I LAY MY REQUESTS* before you and *WAIT.*   (Psalm 5:3)

345

It is good . . . to proclaim your *LOVE* in the
morning. (Psalm 92:1-2)

In the morning my *PRAYER* comes before you.
(Psalm 88:13)

They were . . . every morning to *THANK* and
PRAISE the Lord. (1 Chronicles 23:30)

If you *ASK* and *WAIT, LOVE* and *PRAY, THANK*
and *PRAISE* the Lord each morning, you are bound to
have a wonderful day.

PRAYER:
Lord, thank you for telling me what I must do to have
a good day. Help me to start tomorrow morning.

❧ *TODAY'S DELIGHT:*
As soon as you get up tomorrow morning, start singing:

This is the day, this is the day
That the Lord has made, that the Lord has made.
We will rejoice, we will rejoice
And be glad in it, and be glad in it.
This is the day that the Lord has made;
We will rejoice and be glad in it.
This is the day, this is the day
That the Lord has made. (Based on Psalm 118:24)

If you don't know the tune, ask your parent or Sunday school teacher to sing it for you. Then REJOICE *and* BE GLAD *in the new day.*

Scriptures in this devotion are quoted from the New International Version.

Simon Says!

How can young people keep their way pure? By guarding it according to your word.

(Psalm 119:9 NRSV)

"Simon says, touch your toes. Simon says, turn around."

You've played that game, haven't you? It's a bit like Follow the Leader. You do what "Simon" says, or you lose.

Is there a "Simon" in your life? Somebody who wants you to follow him or her? Are you sure he or she is the right kind of leader?

God did not make you like a robot, operated by push buttons or the sound of a voice. He has given you a special gift—the gift of choice. Sometimes it is difficult to use this gift wisely, because wrong "Simons" make their choices sound exciting.

There is a right "Simon" you can follow, knowing he will never lead you in the wrong direction. This leader's name is Jesus Christ. He wants to teach you how to keep your way "pure" and free from sin. He will always help you to make the right choices as you face any decision in your life.

PRAYER:
Dear Jesus, thank you for giving me such a wonderful gift. Help me to choose your way in everything I do.

&❧ *TODAY'S DELIGHT:*
Play a game of Simon Says.

Names of Jesus

You are to give him the name Jesus. (Matthew 1:21 NIV)

How many different names do you have? Think about this before you answer. Perhaps a boy's full name is William Bruce Jones. Or a girl's name is Elizabeth Marie Thompson. So you may say, "I have three names."

But parents might use the names Bill, Will, or Billy, or for the girl, Liz, Beth, or Bess.

Some children are called by their middle names, or loved ones call them Honey, Son, or Daughter. Grandmother tells others about her "grandson" or "granddaughter," or a girl about her "brother" or "sister." A friend may shout across the playground, "Hi, Buddy!" or "Come here, Smitty!"

Did you know that Jesus had many names? There are even books listing all his names. One such book mentions over 170 names for Jesus. You have heard some of them—Christ, Lord, Savior, and Shepherd. At Christmas, you may hear titles such as Emmanuel, Son of David, King, and Messiah.

Some of Jesus' names are difficult for boys and girls to learn and even pronounce. However, one of his most important names is very easy to remember. That name is "Love." One Christmas carol tells us that "Love was born at Christmas."

350

Whenever you hear the name "Jesus," remember the word *love*. And whenever you think of "love," think of "Jesus."

PRAYER:
Dear Jesus, as I get older, I want to learn more of your names. But for now, help me to remember that your name means "love."

❧ *TODAY'S DELIGHT:*
Write down all the names by which you are called. Don't forget your special nicknames.

Two Hands

Clap your hands, all ye people; shout unto God
with the voice of triumph. (Psalm 47:1)

Are you left-handed or right-handed? Years ago,
left-handed children had a difficult time. Some
teachers tried to make them use their right hands. I
am left-handed, and when I was in school, they did not
have left-handed scissors. I learned to cut with my
right hand; I could also iron clothes with my right
hand. But those are the only two things I do with my
right hand. Today, you can use whichever hand seems
right for you.

But think of all you do with both hands. You help
your family in many ways—raking leaves, drying
dishes, or carrying grocery sacks. You use both
hands for getting dressed and for hugging. You fold
them together to pray. You clap with both hands. The
Bible tells people to clap their hands as a way of
praising God.

Think of this little verse next time you pray:

PRAYER:

Thank you, dear God, for my hands;
I'm glad You gave me two,
For when I use both left and right,
I can do more for You.

352

❧ *TODAY'S DELIGHT:*
Have you ever played finger games using both hands?
Show a younger child how to do:

> *This is the church,*
> *And this is the steeple.*
> *Open the doors,*
> *And see all the people.*

If you're not sure how to make a "church" with your fingers, someone in your church will show you.

Wear a Smile

A happy heart makes the face cheerful.

(Proverbs 15:13 NIV)

Did you know that your face works harder when you frown than when you smile? That's right! It takes more muscles to look angry or sad than it does to look happy!

It may be difficult to smile when you are ill or having a serious problem, although it is possible. But think about all those times you frown because you're crabby or lose your temper.

You may ask, "How can I be happy when I'm angry with a friend? Or when my little sister tattles on me? How can I smile when I have to miss my favorite television show to do homework?"

Another version of the Bible states the above verse this way: "When people are happy, they smile" (TEV).

If you start each day with pleasant thoughts and words, you will feel better inside. When you feel better inside, you'll want to smile. Then, before you know it, your face will reflect the way you feel in your heart. The result? A great day!

PRAYER:
Dear Father, help me to be a cheerful person and to start each day with a smile and a happy "Good morning!"

✦ *TODAY'S DELIGHT:*
Smile at everyone you meet today. If you don't get a smile in return, say a little prayer for that person. You may be surprised at the results.

Setting a Good Example

Don't let anyone look down on you because you are young, but set an example. (1 Timothy 4:12 NIV)

Have you ever skipped a stone on the surface of a lake or pond? How many times did it skip? Did you notice that each skip causes ripples to spread out on the water's surface? Did you watch the ripples travel across the water for some distance?

Think of yourself as that skipping stone. Every time you meet someone, it is like the stone touching the water. No matter how old you are, you leave ripples in other people's lives. They may consist of love or hate, joy or sadness, right or wrong.

Your ripples may influence people all day. What you say or do may even travel with them the rest of their lives!

It's up to you to decide what kind of example you will be to your friends, your teachers, and your family. This is a great responsibility and God wants to help you with it every day. You need only ask him.

PRAYER:
God, I want to make ripples of love and joy in the lives of others. I want to do what is right. Please help me.

Setting a Good Example

TODAY'S DELIGHT:
*Think of a specific kind of "ripple" you can be in some-
one else's life today (or tomorrow, if you're reading this
in the evening). Perhaps you can do someone a favor
such as running an errand, helping with a difficult
chore, or saying cheerful words to someone who is
unhappy.*

357

Keeping Promises

The LORD is faithful to all his promises and loving toward all he has made. (Psalm 145:13 NIV)

Did you promise to come home right after school, but spent too much time on the playground? Or did you promise Mom you'd empty the garbage before you left in the morning and then forgot? How about the promise to play a game with your little sister, but you decided to go to a friend's house instead?

Did a friend ever break a promise to you? How did you feel? Angry? Sad? If we want to have friends and earn our parents' trust, we must try to keep promises.

Keeping promises is an important part of growing up. If Dad were always late for work, he might lose his job; or if he decided not to fix your bike tire after he'd promised, you might be very upset. If your mom decided she didn't feel like food shopping or cooking for a week, you might get quite hungry. These are the kinds of promises your parents have made.

God knows you may slip once in a while, but if you ask, he will forgive you. That's something you can count on because God never breaks a promise! Isn't that wonderful?

PRAYER:
Thank you, God, for loving me and always keeping your promises. Help me to keep my promises too.

&❧ *TODAY'S DELIGHT:*
Think of something you've promised a family member—perhaps your parents, or your brother or sister. Or maybe you've made a promise to a friend. Follow through with your word of honor (that's what a promise is!). The receiver will be delighted, and you will be too!

Heavy Burdens

Carry each other's burdens.   (Galatians 6:2 NIV)

Have you ever seen a horse carrying a load? Or maybe a person with an armful of packages? Perhaps you've watched an elephant, camel, or donkey on television with huge bundles on its back.

These animals are all carrying physical burdens. What does it mean when the Bible tells us to "carry each other's burdens"? Should we help others carry their packages? That's a helpful idea, but some burdens don't even weigh an ounce.

You may have a friend who is sad because her grandmother died. Grief is your friend's burden. Or your brother may be angry because his best friend made an unkind remark. Anger is a terrible burden to carry. Others may feel guilty because they sassed their mother or fibbed to their teacher. Guilt is also a heavy load.

How can you carry another's burdens? You can invite friends to Sunday school, or introduce them to an adult Christian who can talk with them about their burdens.

But best of all, you can tell them that Jesus is a great burden-carrier. He will not only carry these heavy loads, but he can remove them altogether. Remember this, too, when *you* are carrying a burden.

PRAYER:
Dear God, I want to help my friends in their troubles.
And I sometimes need help with my own burdens.
Thank you for being there whenever I need you.

🕊 *TODAY'S DELIGHT:*
Surprise your mom and offer to carry a burden (the garbage, the groceries from the car, clean clothes to everyone's room).

Be Kind to One Another

Always try to be kind to each other and to everyone else. (1 Thessalonians 5:15 NIV)

Are there children in your school or classroom who don't speak English well? Perhaps their native language is Spanish, Korean, or Vietnamese. It's very difficult to learn a new language, especially if it is not spoken in one's home.

Over two hundred years ago, a boy was born to parents who had come from Holland to live in the United States. They spoke only Dutch in the home. The boy often had to help his father, so he couldn't go to school regularly. But he worked very hard to learn English and to do well in his studies. That boy's name was Martin Van Buren, and he became the eighth president of the United States.

Children from foreign lands may grow up to serve our country in many ways. These boys and girls want to be good citizens. You can help them by becoming a friend. Speak slowly so they can learn English words. Be patient as you try to understand what they are saying. Above all, be kind and show them God's love.

PRAYER:
Dear God, you love everyone. Help me to be friendly to people from other countries.

🕊 *TODAY'S DELIGHT:*
Ask your parents or grandparents if you may invite a
new friend from another country to play with you, or
perhaps to enjoy a meal or evening with your family.

A New Pet

A righteous man cares for the needs of his animal.

(Proverbs 12:10 NIV)

"Mom, may I have a dog?" Jerry couldn't keep his eyes off the picture of a floppy-eared dog and the words, "I need a good home!"

"A dog is a lot of work, Jerry."

"I'd take care of him. Honest, I would!"

Many children, like Jerry, have the best intentions. But after a few days, they forget their promise. Then Mom or Dad must take over the responsibilities.

Just as you need food and water every day, so a pet must receive proper food and water daily. If your dog is tied up, he requires periods of exercise. Unlike cats, dogs do not use a litter box. So you may need to clean up dog waste in your backyard, which is a very unpleasant chore.

If you choose a cat, she cannot be allowed to sharpen her claws on Mother's furniture. Gerbils must have their cages cleaned out regularly, and fish need clean aquariums.

God has created many wonderful animals for pets, but unlike wild creatures, tame animals need proper care. If you have a pet, make sure you can be trusted to do your part.

PRAYER:
Dear God, help me to do my best in caring for my pet.

  ❧ *TODAY'S DELIGHT:*
Show special love to your pet today. Exercise your dog or play with your cat. If you don't have a pet, perhaps you can offer to care for your neighbors' animal when they are gone on vacation or for the weekend.

Clouds

*See! He is arriving, surrounded by clouds; and
every eye shall see him.*   (Revelation 1:7 TLB)

Have you ever lain on your back and watched the
clouds? Did you see interesting shapes and designs?
God has made different kinds of clouds.

Nimbus clouds are dark and gray, bringing us much
needed rain. *Cirrus* clouds appear very high in the
sky and look like wispy curls of smoke. Gray foglike
layers close to the earth are likely to be *stratus* clouds.
They resemble smooth sheets, with drizzle often
falling from them. The piled-up masses of fluffy
clouds floating by on a summer's day are *cumulus*
clouds. Sometimes when a cumulus cloud rises
thousands of feet, it may mean a thunderstorm.

All clouds consist of water drops and ice crystals.
The water they bring in the form of rain and snow is
necessary for all living creatures.

The Bible tells us that the Lord Jesus will one day
return to earth on the clouds. We don't know which
kind of clouds, but that's not important. What's
important is that everyone who is living on earth will
see him. Isn't that exciting?

PRAYER:
Thank you, God, for clouds to give us moisture.
Thank you that Jesus will come back someday on one
of your clouds.

❧ *TODAY'S DELIGHT:*
If the weather is nice, lie outside on your back and
watch the clouds. What do their shapes remind you of?
Try to identify the different kinds of clouds.

God Made the Dark

You will not fear the terror of night. (Psalm 91:5 NIV)

Jeremy did not like bedtime. He enjoyed taking a bath, and the Bible stories Mother or Dad read to him. But do you know why Jeremy disliked bedtime? He was afraid of the dark!

One evening his mother took him by the hand and led him outside. They sat down in lawn chairs in the middle of the yard.

"Listen, Jeremy. Do you hear that noise?" It was the sound of a bird cooing in the distance. "That's a mother bird telling her babies it's time to settle down in the nest and sleep."

Mother pointed to a flower. "Does this flower look different than it did this morning when we weeded the garden?"

"It's smaller now than in the daytime," said Jeremy. He thought for a while. "Oh, flowers must sleep by folding up their petals!"

Suddenly Jeremy heard his dog bark. "Brownie wonders who is out in the yard. It's only Mom and me, Brownie," he called.

"It's Brownie's bedtime too, Jeremy. You see, God provides darkness for the animals and flowers too. All living things need rest as well as food to make them grow."

Jeremy thought about that. Then he took Mother's hand again and said, "I think I'm ready for bed now."

"Let's thank God for his plan for rest, shall we?" Mother and Jeremy bowed their heads while Brownie barked a "Good night."

PRAYER:
Thank you, God, for the dark so that animals, flowers, and people can get a good night's sleep. Help me not to be afraid.

๕ *TODAY'S DELIGHT:*
Ask a family member to go outside with you after dark. Look at the stars. Listen for special night sounds. Then go to bed without complaining or being afraid.

Are You Afraid?

Perfect love drives out fear.   (1 John 4:18 NIV)

Are you afraid of something right now? Maybe it's the big dog that barks at you when you ride your bike to school. It may be a dark hallway outside your bedroom.

Or is your fear about other people? Perhaps you heard your parents arguing and you're afraid they may get a divorce. Or you may have a sick relative and you're afraid he or she may die.

You don't need to be ashamed of your fears. Adults have them too. God knows your fears—the big ones and the little ones. He not only knows them, but more important, he wants to help you get rid of them.

The Bible says perfect love will drive out fear. What does that mean? Ask yourself these questions. Can I be up in a tree (or flying in a plane) and be on the ground at the same time? Can I be at school and at home at the same time? Of course not. In the same way, love and fear cannot live together. If you ask Jesus to remind you that he is with you every day and remember his love for you, the fear will disappear.

So whenever ugly fear fills your mind or your body, just take it to Jesus, and see what a difference it makes.

PRAYER:
Thank you, Jesus, for your love, which will chase away my fears.

🕊 *TODAY'S DELIGHT:*
Here's a "mind game" to play whenever you feel afraid.
Start with the letter A and think of a word that
describes God. Perhaps awesome or ageless. Then the
letter B—best or beautiful. Go through the alphabet,
and before you know it, those fearful thoughts will be
gone. (Hint: For X, use words like eXcellent.)

A Family Altar

Then Noah built an altar to the LORD.

(Genesis 8:20 NIV)

So he [Abraham] built an altar there to the LORD.

(Genesis 12:7 NIV)

As soon as his family and the animals left the ark, Noah built an altar. Abraham built an altar after he arrived in a new land, even before he put up a tent for his family.

An altar is a special place used to worship God. Ancient altars were built of earth or stone. Church altars may be made of wood, metal, or stone.

Many homes today have family altars. A Bible and perhaps a wooden or iron cross are set on a table or stand. The table might be covered with a pretty cloth and a candle placed on it.

A family altar is a gathering place for parents and children to have devotions. A person may also go to the altar to pray alone or with another family member. The family altar reminds us of God's wonderful love.

PRAYER:
Dear God, thank you for family altars that help us to worship you in our homes.

&ᴥ *Today's Delight:*
Ask your mother or father to help you find a special spot in your home for a family altar. If this is impossible, try to set one up in a corner of your bedroom, or even on a nightstand next to your bed. Place appropriate items on your altar.

The Best Book of All

They . . . examined the Scriptures every day.

(Acts 17:11 NIV)

"What did you do this summer?" asked Mrs. Blake. All the children in the Sunday school class began to talk at once.

"One at a time," she said, laughing. "What did you do, Bill?"

"My family camped in the mountains. I caught lots of fish!"

"We camped all across the United States," said Mary Ann.

Tracy told about a visit with her grandparents. "I helped my grandma in the garden and my grandpa with the cows."

"I went to Australia and Japan and to the moon." Everybody stared at Alex.

Mrs. Blake said, "I think you're fooling us, Alex!"

"I did go to those places—in books! My dad didn't get a vacation this year, so I read books about Australia, Japan, the moon, and lots of other places!"

Like Alex, we can visit many places in our mind through the books we read. We can even travel to the Holy Land where Jesus lived. When we use our imagination, we understand more of the Bible. It is the most exciting Book that has ever been written.

PRAYER:
Thank you, Father, for my wonderful mind. As I grow older, help me to learn more about you by reading the Bible.

🕊 *TODAY'S DELIGHT:*
Check at your library (perhaps your church has a library) for a book about the Holy Land or about your favorite Bible character. Share what you learn with a friend.

Delight in the ABCs

A

AGE

Cast me not off in the time of old AGE; forsake me not when my strength faileth. PSALM 71:9

AGE, I make light of it,
Fear not the sight of it,
Time's but a playmate, whose toys are divine.

—THOMAS WENTWORTH HIGGINSON

B

BATTLE

The BATTLE is the LORD's. 1 SAMUEL 17:47

The BATTLE, sir, is not to the strong alone; it is to the vigilant, the active, the brave. —PATRICK HENRY

C

CROSS

If any want to become my followers, let them deny themselves and take up their CROSS and follow me.

MATTHEW 16:24 NRSV

There are no crown-wearers in heaven who were not
CROSS-bearers here below.

—CHARLES HADDON SPURGEON

D

DAY/DAYS
May your strength match the length of your DAYS!

DEUTERONOMY 33:25 TLB

Every DAY is a fresh beginning.
Every morn is the world made new.

—SARAH CHAUNCEY WOOLSEY

E

ETERNITY
He has also set ETERNITY in the hearts of men.

ECCLESIASTES 3:11 NIV

ETERNITY is not something that begins after you are
dead. It is going on all the time. We are in it now.

—CHARLOTTE PERKINS GILMAN

F

FEAR
*Do not FEAR, for I am with you, do not be afraid, for I
am your God.*

ISAIAH 41:10 NRSV

The only thing we have to FEAR is FEAR itself.

—FRANKLIN D. ROOSEVELT

G

GRACE

My GRACE is sufficient for you, for my power is made perfect in weakness. 2 CORINTHIANS 12:9 NIV

When GRACE is joined with wrinkles, it is adorable.

—VICTOR HUGO

H

HEALTH

For I will restore HEALTH to you, and your wounds I will heal, says the LORD. JEREMIAH 30:17 NRSV

Look to your HEALTH; and if you have it, praise God, and value it next to a good conscience; for HEALTH is the second blessing that we mortals are capable of; a blessing that money cannot buy. —IZAAK WALTON

I

INFINITE

Great is our Lord, and of great power: his understanding is INFINITE. PSALM 147:5

The Indian summer of life should be a little sunny,
and a little sad, like the season, and INFINITE in
wealth and depth of tone, but never hustled.

—HENRY BROOKS ADAMS

J

JOY

For the JOY of the LORD is your strength.

NEHEMIAH 8:10 NRSV

If you have no JOY in your religion, there's a leak in
your Christianity somewhere. —W. A. "BILLY" SUNDAY

K

KINDNESS

*Clothe yourselves with compassion, KINDNESS,
humility, gentleness and patience.* COLOSSIANS 3:12 NIV

Better to do a KINDNESS at home than walk a
thousand miles to burn incense. —THE DEFENDER

L

LOVE

*God is LOVE, and those who abide in LOVE abide in
God, and God abides in them. . . . We LOVE because he
first loved us.* 1 JOHN 4:16, 19 NRSV

Those who LOVE deeply never grow old; they may die of old age, but they die young.

—SIR ARTHUR WING PINERO

M

MERCY

He has showed you, O man, what is good. And what does the LORD require of you? To act justly and to love MERCY and to walk humbly with your God. MICAH 6:8 NIV

Teach me to feel another's woe,
To hide the fault I see;
That MERCY I to others show,
That MERCY show to me. —ALEXANDER POPE

N

NEIGHBOR

You shall love the Lord your God with all your heart, and with all your soul, and with all your strength, and with all your mind; and your NEIGHBOR as yourself. LUKE 10:27 NRSV

When your NEIGHBOR's house is afire, your own property is at stake. —HORACE

O

OLD

Even to your OLD age I am he, even when you turn gray I will carry you. I have made, and I will bear; I will carry and will save. ISAIAH 46:4 NRSV

Grow OLD along with me!
The best is yet to be,
The last of life for which the first was made . . .

—ROBERT BROWNING

P

PRAY

Evening, and morning, and at noon, will I PRAY, and cry aloud: and he shall hear my voice. PSALM 55:17

Work as if you were to live 100 years; PRAY as if you were to die tomorrow. —BENJAMIN FRANKLIN

Q

QUIET/QUIETNESS

Only in returning to me and waiting for me will you be saved; in QUIETNESS and confidence is your strength. ISAIAH 30:15 TLB

Give us grace and strength to forbear and to persevere. Give us courage and gaiety and the QUIET

mind, spare to us our friends, soften to us our
enemies.   —ROBERT LOUIS STEVENSON

R

REVERENCE

REVERENCE for God adds hours to each day.

PROVERBS 10:27 TLB

I have in my heart a small shy plant called
REVERENCE; I cultivate that on Sunday mornings.

—OLIVER WENDELL HOLMES, SR.

S

STRENGTH

*They that wait upon the LORD shall renew their
STRENGTH.*   ISAIAH 40:31

Nothing is so strong as gentleness;
nothing so gentle as real STRENGTH.

—ST. FRANCIS DE SALES

T

TRUTH

*You will know the TRUTH, and the TRUTH will make
you free.*   JOHN 8:32 NRSV

It fortifies my soul to know
That, though I perish, TRUTH is so.

—ARTHUR HUGH CLOUGH

U

UNDERSTAND/UNDERSTANDS

But true wisdom and power are God's. He alone knows
what we should do; he UNDERSTANDS.

JOB 12:13 TLB

Let us have faith that right makes might; and in that
faith let us to the end dare to do our duty as we
UNDERSTAND it. —ABRAHAM LINCOLN

V

VIRTUOUS

Who can find a VIRTUOUS woman? For her price is
far above rubies. PROVERBS 31:10

Age in a VIRTUOUS person of either sex, carries in it
an authority which makes it preferable to all the
pleasures of youth. —SIR RICHARD STEELE

W

WORDS

Heaven and earth will pass away, but my words will not
pass away. MARK 13:31 NRSV

For of all sad WORDS of tongue or pen,
The saddest are these: "It might have been!"

—JOHN GREENLEAF WHITTIER

X

EXPECTATION

*My soul, wait thou only upon God; for my
EXPECTATION is from him.*   PSALM 62:5

'Tis EXPECTATION make a blessing dear,
Heaven were not heaven, if we knew what it were.

—SIR JOHN SUCKLING

Y

YEARS

*But do not forget this one thing, dear friends: With the
Lord a day is like a thousand YEARS, and a thousand
YEARS are like a day.*   2 PETER 3:8 NIV

O God, our help in ages past,
Our hope for YEARS to come,
Our shelter from the stormy blast,
And our eternal home.   —ISAAC WATTS

387

Z

ZEAL

My ZEAL for God and his work burns hot within me.

PSALM 69:9 TLB

Nothing can be fairer or more noble than the holy fervor of true ZEAL. —JEAN BAPTISTE MOLIÉRE